DUE DATE **MCN**	03/10	21.99
JUN 16 2010	FEB 27 2012	
	MAR 19 2012	
SEP 27 2010	AUG 14 2013	
OCT 05 2011		
OCT NOV 16 22 2011		
NOV 12 2011		
Nov. 28, 2011		
APR 15 2013		

END

THE

FED

END
THE
FED

Ron Paul

GRAND CENTRAL
PUBLISHING

NEW YORK   BOSTON

Grand Central Publishing
Hachette Book Group
237 Park Avenue
New York, NY 10017

Visit our Web site at www.HachetteBookGroup.com.

Printed in the United States of America

First Edition: September 2009
10 9 8 7 6 5 4 3

Grand Central Publishing is a division of Hachette Book Group, Inc.
The Grand Central Publishing name and logo is a trademark of Hachette
Book Group, Inc.

Library of Congress Cataloging-in-Publication Data
Paul, Ron
    End the Fed / Ron Paul.—1st ed.
        p.   cm.
        ISBN 978-0-446-54919-6 (regular edition)—ISBN 978-0-446-55997-3
    (large print edition)
        1. Board of Governors of the Federal Reserve System (U.S.)
    2. Federal Reserve banks.   3. Monetary policy—United States.
    4. Banks and banking, Central—United States.   I. Title.
    HG2563.P384   2009
    332.1'10973—dc22
                                                    2009024804

*To the young people who powered my presidential campaign
and who are the heart of the anti-Fed movement.*

In your hands is the hope of a free and prosperous society.

ACKNOWLEDGMENTS

My first thanks go to my wife, Carol, whose love and support make possible everything I do. And without my great teachers in Austrian economics—Ludwig von Mises, Murray N. Rothbard, F. A. Hayek, Henry Hazlitt, and Hans F. Sennholz—this book would not exist.

Thanks also to my editor Ben Greenberg, for his most effective help.

Contents

END
THE
FED

CHAPTER 1

WHY YOU SHOULD CARE

Everybody thinks about money and almost everybody wants more. We use money without thinking much about its nature and function. Few of us ask where it comes from, who controls it, why it has value, or why it loses value from time to time.

In the same way, most people accept the Federal Reserve—the manager of the nation's money stock—as an indispensable institution that the United States cannot function without, and so they don't question it. But I assure you, especially in this post-meltdown world, that it is irresponsible, ineffective, and ultimately useless to have a serious economic debate without considering fundamental issues about money and its quality, as well as the Fed's massive role in manipulating money to our economic ruin.

What is the Fed and what does it do? To answer these questions, you can read books, study pamphlets issued by the Fed, or attend economics lectures at your local college. You can even consult the Fed's comic books on its own Web site.[1] You

1. http://www.newyorkfed.org/publications/result.cfm?comics=1.

will be told how the Fed serves to stabilize the business cycle, control inflation, maintain a solvent banking system, regulate the financial system, and more. Certainly, the Fed's spokesmen claim that they do all this and do it well.

I disagree on each point.

After all is said and done, the Fed has one power that is unique to it alone: it enables the creation of money out of thin air. Sometimes it makes vast new amounts. Sometimes it makes lesser amounts. The money takes a variety of forms and enters the system in various ways. And the Fed does this through techniques such as open-market operations, changing reserve ratios, and manipulating interest rates, operations that all result in money creation.

Given that money is one half of every commercial transaction and that whole civilizations literally rise and fall based on the quality of their money, we are talking about an awesome power, one that flies under cover of night. It is the power to weave illusions that appear real as long as they last. That is the very core of the Fed's power.

As President Barack Obama said of the economic boom that went bust: "I think it's important to understand that some of that wealth was illusory in the first place."[2]

Exactly.

But let's also understand the source of the illusion and what to do about it.

Of course, not everyone is instinctively against this illusion-

---

2. "After the Great Recession," interview with President Obama, *New York Times Magazine*, April 28, 2009 (conducted by David Leonhardt).

weaving power, and many even welcome it. They just want to get back to the times when "everything was good" even though it was all just a mirage—a creation of the appearance of wealth by the Fed.

It is frequently thought that relieving an alleged shortage of money will solve all social problems. Even today, with an economic crisis raging, the response by our government and the Federal Reserve has been characteristic. Interest rates are driven to zero and trillions of dollars are pushed into the economy with no evidence that any problems will be solved. The authorities remain oblivious to the fact that they are only making our problems worse in the long run.

Economic booms and busts have been around for a long time. Tragically, the innocent who understand little about the complexity of the monetary system suffer the most, while those who are in the know reap great profits whether the market is going up or down. Only an understanding of how the monetary system works can correct this problem and protect the victims caught in a vicious economic downturn.

Everyone should have an intense interest in what money is and how it's manipulated by the few at the expense of the many. Money is crucial for survival. It is necessary for maintaining a free society. A healthy economy depends on it. Limiting political power is impossible without it. Sound money is essential for preventing unnecessary wars. Prosperity and peace in the long run are impossible without it.

To understand money, one absolutely must understand what a central bank is all about. In the United States, the central bank is the Federal Reserve, the instrument by which our money and credit are constantly manipulated for the benefit of a privileged class.

I've written this book to explain why I think the system of Fed domination must come to an end. I've been speaking and writing on this subject for more than thirty years, but there was a time when hardly anyone cared what I had to say about this subject. The economic crisis has changed everything. Today there is a growing social movement, even a political movement, dedicated to ending the Fed.

In fact, the title of this book is not my own but rather comes from a slogan that can be heard at rallies all around the country. I first heard it at the University of Michigan in October 2007, after the Republican primary debate in Dearborn. It was a frustrating evening; all my opponents denied there was anything at all wrong with the economy or Bush administration policies. But afterward, I was able to speak to more than 4,000 students in the quad at Ann Arbor.

I'm told that was a big turnout for a candidate. And it was a very friendly crowd, applauding my comments on government spending and deficits and on wars and foreign policy. But when I mentioned monetary policy, the kids started cheering. Then a small group chanted, "End the Fed! End the Fed!" The whole crowd took up the call. Many held up burning dollar bills, as if to say to the central bank, you have done enough damage to the American people, our future, and to the world: your time is up.

Then, in September 2008, at my counterconvention in Minneapolis, 12,000 people started the chant long before I even mentioned the issue of the Fed. I laughed and said, "Wait a minute!" But they did not, for money, its quality and future, is surely the issue of our times.

I've always been an optimist about the cause of sound money, but even I never imagined that the anti-Fed cause would become material for popular protests in my lifetime. All around the country, people are gathering outside Federal Reserve buildings to protest against the power, secrecy, and operations of the Fed, and chanting this great slogan. Their goal is not reform but revolution: an end to the Fed.

I'm thrilled. You should be, too, since ending the Fed would be the single greatest step we could take to restoring American prosperity and freedom and guaranteeing that they both have a future.

I have no doubt that some people consider such protests to be shocking, radical, even dangerous, but the truth is that they arise from an impulse deeply rooted in our nation's history. The nineteenth century saw many similar protests against the national bank system and the attempt to centralize money and credit in a government-sponsored, government-backed institution that operates in complete secrecy.

One might say that this is a populist cause. It is also a libertarian cause, one that would be cheered by Thomas Jefferson, a dedicated opponent of the Fed's predecessor, the Bank of the United States, and by Thomas Paine, who saw paper money as the enemy of individual liberty on grounds that it always gives rise to despotism.

Paine, the same writer who inspired the American Revolution with his pamphlet *Common Sense*, also said this: "As to the assumed authority of any assembly in making paper money, or paper of any kind, a legal tender, or in other language, a compulsive payment, it is a most presumptuous attempt at arbitrary power. There can be no such power in a republican government: the people have no freedom—and property no security—where this practice can be acted."[3]

In the same way, there were great opponents of central banking despotism in the nineteenth century, and entire presidential elections turned on the question of whether there should be a national bank of note issue.

Indeed, opposition to a money monopoly has roots all the way back to the fourteenth century in the work of the earliest economists who thought about the dangers of inflation.[4]

This cause is also justified in the work of the finest economists and philosophers of the twentieth century. Nobel laureate F. A. Hayek, for example, wrote of central banking: "I doubt whether it has ever done any good except to the rulers and their favorites," and he concluded that "money is certainly too dangerous an instrument to leave to the fortuitous expediency of politicians."[5]

It is and should be a mainstream cause to end the power and secrecy of the Fed. It's my own view that ending the Fed would address the most vexing problems of politics of our time. It would bring an end to dollar depreciation. It would take away from the government the means to fund its endless wars. It would curb the government's attacks on the civil lib-

3. *The Complete Writings of Thomas Paine*, Philip Foner, ed. (New York: Citadel Press, 1945), pp. 405ff.

4. Jörg Guido Hülsmann, *The Ethics of Money Production* (Auburn, AL: Mises Institute, 2008).

5. F. A. Hayek, *Choice in Currency* (London: Institute of Economic Affairs, 1976), p. 16.

erties of Americans, stop its vast debt accumulation that will be paid by future generations, and arrest its massive expansions of the welfare state that has turned us into a nation of dependents.

If you solve the money monopoly problem by ending the Fed, you solve many other problems, too. Essentially you take away from the government the capacity to use financial trickery to expand without limit. It is the first step to restoring constitutional government. Without the Fed, the federal government would have to live within its means. It would still be too big and too intrusive, just like all state governments are today, but the outrageous empire at home and abroad would have to come to an end.

There are other benefits as well, such as stopping the business cycle, ending inflation, building prosperity for all Americans, and putting an end to the corrupt collaboration between government and banks that virtually defines the operations of public policy in the post-meltdown era.

Ending the Fed would put the American banking system on solid financial footing. The industry would thrive without the moral hazard of banks that are "too big to fail." Its loan operations would take a more realistic account of risks, and the bank's capital would not be put at risk in the service of politically driven priorities.

Customers' deposits would be safer than they are today, as banks would compete with one another in their most important function of providing a secure means of preserving wealth.

Ending the Fed would also end the way in which our election cycles have been corrupted by monetary manipulation. No longer would presidents be in a position to lean on the central bank to artificially boost the economy before elections, only to have a recession hit after the party in power is sworn in again.

The national wealth would no longer be hostage to the whims of a handful of appointed bureaucrats whose interests are equally divided between serving the banking cartel and serving the most powerful politicians in Washington.

Ending the Fed is the one sure way to restore sanity to economic and political life in this country. It doesn't mean that our political disagreements and fights in Congress will go away. Ending the Fed is not a magic pill to usher in Utopia. But it does mean that our disagreements and discussions will occur within the context of reality, not in the illusory world created by the unlimited printing of money.

The time to do it is now. The Fed's activities since the market meltdown of 2008 have been dangerous in the extreme. The Fed is using all its power to drive the monetary base to unprecedented heights, creating trillions in new money out of thin air. From April 2008 to April 2009, the adjusted monetary base shot up from $856 billion to an unbelievable $1.749 trillion. Was there any new wealth created? New production? No, this was the Ben Bernanke printing press at work. If you and I did anything similar, we would be called counterfeiters and be sent away for a lifetime in prison. We would be scorned and hated by everyone as scam artists and racketeers. But when the Fed does it—complete with a scientific gloss—it is seen as the perfectly legal and responsible conduct of monetary policy.

This new money now sits as reserves in bank vaults awaiting a safe environment for lending and borrowing. Should

St. Louis Adjusted Monetary Base (BASE)

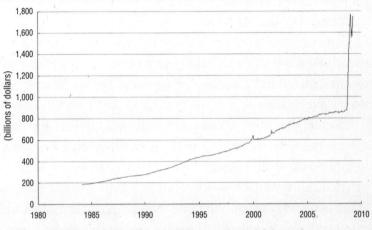

Source: Federal Reserve Bank of St. Louis: 2009 research.stlouisfed.org

that safe environment arrive, we could see a level of price increases none of us have experienced in our lifetime.

Some people think the experience of the Weimar Republic in Germany in the interwar years, when paper money was made so worthless by the central bank that the bills were literally used as fuel to heat homes, is entirely impossible in the United States.

We think we are immune from such a calamity, but we are not.

Bad economic policy can destroy a civilization—no policy is more dangerous than bad monetary policy. After decades of experience in grappling with Fed officials in committee meetings and of lunches and private discussions with Fed chairmen, a lifetime of reading serious economic literature, and a profound awareness of the dangers to liberty in our time, I know there is absolutely no hope for the Fed to conduct responsible monetary policy.

We need to take away the government's money power. The banking industry needs its welfare check ended. The dollar's soundness depends on its being untied from the machine that can make an infinite number of copies of dollars and reduce their value to zero.

The fact that the Fed can create trillions of dollars and distribute them to its cronies without congressional oversight should shock us all. I thought I was immune to being shocked by what our government does, but the actions of the Fed in 2008–2009 went beyond the pale. Not only did the Fed create many trillions of dollars and pass them out, it refused to explain its actions. This shows the arrogance of the members of the Fed and the complete apathy of the Congress in assuming its responsibility to protect the people and follow the law.

Back on November 21, 2002, Ben Bernanke explained precisely what his views are, so perhaps there should have been no surprise.[6]

The U.S. government has a technology, called a printing press (or, today, its electronic equivalent), that allows it to produce as many U.S. dollars as it wishes at essentially no cost. By increasing the number of U.S. dollars in circulation, or even by credibly threatening to do so, the U.S. government can also reduce the value of a dollar in terms of goods and services, which is equivalent to rais-

6. Remarks by Governor Ben S. Bernanke before the National Economists Club, Washington, D.C., November 21, 2002.

ing the prices in dollars of those goods and services. We conclude that, under a paper-money system, a determined government can always generate higher spending and hence positive inflation.

I'm not sure that the Fed governor has ever been so frank about the Fed's power. To be sure, he was not condemning it. He was explaining it. He believes in it. Like the eighteenth-century money crank, John Law, whose antics fueled the Mississippi Bubble, Bernanke believes he has discovered the magic means to generate prosperity.[7]

Rarely does an opportunity present itself to interest the average person in the monetary system enough to demand reform, but one is now upon us. Although we face a crisis, we have an excellent opportunity to strike a blow for freedom, which cannot exist without sound money.

The Federal Reserve System must be challenged. Ultimately, it needs to be eliminated. The government cannot and should not be trusted with a monopoly on money. No single institution in society should have power this immense. In fact, I believe that freedom itself is at stake in this struggle.

7. Doug French, *Early Speculative Bubbles and Increases in the Supply of Money* (Auburn, AL: Mises Institute, 2009).

CHAPTER 2

THE ORIGIN AND NATURE OF THE FED

Most Americans haven't thought much about the strange entity that controls the nation's money. They simply accept it as though it has always been there, which is far from the case. Visitors to Washington can see the Fed's palatial headquarters in Washington, D.C., which opened its doors in 1937. Tourists observe its intimidating appearance and forbidding structure, the monetary parallel to the Supreme Court of the capital of the United States.

People know that this institution has an important job to do in managing the nation's money supply, and they hear the head of the Fed testify to Congress, citing complex data, making predictions, and attempting to intimidate anyone who would take issue with them. One would never suspect from their words that there is any mismanagement taking place. The head of the Fed always postures as a master of the universe, someone completely knowledgeable and completely in control.

But how much do we really know about what goes on inside the Fed? With the newest round of bailouts, even journalists have a difficult time running down precisely where the money is coming from and where it is headed. From its founding in 1913, secrecy and inside deals have been part of the way the Fed works.

Part of the public relations game played by the chairman of the Fed is designed to suggest that the Fed is an essential part of our system, one we cannot do without. In fact, the Fed came about during a period of our nation's history called the Progressive Era, when the income tax and many new government institutions were created. It was a time in which business in general became infatuated with the idea of forming cartels as a way of protecting profits and socializing losses.

The largest banks were no exception. They were very unhappy that there was no national lender of last resort that they could depend on to bail them out in times of crisis. With no bailout mechanism in place, they had to sink or swim on their own merits. What was more, following the Civil War, American presidents worked to implement and defend the gold standard, which put a brake on the ability of the largest banks to expand credit without limit. The gold standard worked like a regulator in this way. Ultimately, banks had to function like every other business. They could expand and make risky loans up to a point, but when faced with bankruptcy, they had nowhere to turn. They would have to contract loans and deal with extreme financial pressures. Risk bearing is a wonderful mechanism for regulating human decision making. This created a culture of lending discipline.

In the jargon of the day, the system lacked "elasticity." That's another way of saying that banks couldn't expand money and credit as much as they wanted. They couldn't inflate without limit and count on a centralized institution to bail them out. This agenda fit well with a growing political movement at the turn of the twentieth century that favored inflation (sometimes summed up in the slogan "Free Silver") as a means of relieving the debt burden of farmers. The cause took on certain populist overtones, and many people began to believe that an elastic money supply would help the common man. They identified the gold standard as a system favored by large banks to keep credit tight. Even today, many writers on the Fed mistakenly believe that the central bank and the largest banks are working to keep credit tight in their own interest.

Even the Fed itself claims that part of its job is to keep inflation in check. This is something like the tobacco industry claiming that it is trying to stop smoking or the automobile industry claiming that it is trying to control road congestion. The Fed is in the business of generating inflation. It might attempt to stop the *effects* of inflation, namely, rising prices. But under the old definition of inflation—an artificial increase in the supply of money and credit—the entire reason for the Fed's existence is to generate more, not less, of it.

What the largest banks desire is precisely what we might expect any large corporation to desire: privatized profits and socialized losses. The privatized profits come from successful loan activities, sometimes during economic booms. But when the boom turns to bust, the losses are absorbed by third parties and do not affect the bottom line. To cover losses requires a supply of money that stretches to meet bankers' demands. This is something that every industry would like if they could get it. But it is something that the free market denies them, and rightly so.

The banking industry has always had trouble with the idea of a free market that provides opportunities for both profits and losses. The first part, the industry likes. The second part is another issue. That is the reason for the constant drive in American history toward the centralization of money and banking, a trend that not only benefits the largest banks with the most to lose from a sound money system, but also the government, which is able to use an elastic system as an alternative form of revenue support. The coalition of government and big bankers provides the essential backbone of support for the centralization of money and credit.

If we look at banking history, we see that the drive for centralization of power dates back centuries. Whenever instability turns up, so do efforts to socialize the losses. Rarely do people ask what the fundamental source of instability really is. For an answer we can turn to a monumental study published in 2006 by Spanish economist Jesús Huerta de Soto.[1] He places the blame on the very institution of fractional-reserve banking, the notion that depositors' money currently in use as cash may also be loaned out for speculative projects and then redeposited. The system works so long as people do not attempt to withdraw all their money at once, as permitted to them in the banking contract. Once they do attempt this, the bank faces a choice to go bankrupt or suspend payment. In the face of such a demand, a bank turns to other banks to provide liquidity. But when the failure becomes systemwide, it turns to the government.

---

1. Jesús Huerta de Soto, *Money, Bank Credit, Economic Cycles* (Auburn, AL: Mises Institute, 2006).

The core of the problem is the conglomeration of two distinct functions of a bank. The first is the warehousing function, the most traditional function of a bank. The bank keeps your money safe and provides services such as checking, ATM access, record keeping, and online payment methods. These are all part of the warehousing services of the bank, and they are services for which the consumer is traditionally asked to pay (unless costs can be recouped through some other means). The second service the bank provides is a loan service. It seeks out investments such as commercial ventures and real estate and puts money at risk in search of a rate of return. People who want their money put into such ventures are choosing to accept risk and hoping for a return, understanding that if the investments do not work out, they lose money in the process.

The institution of fractional reserves mixes these two functions, such that warehousing becomes a source for lending. The bank loans out money that has been warehoused and stands ready to use in checking accounts or other forms of checkable deposits, and that newly loaned money is deposited yet again in checkable deposits. It is loaned out again and deposited, with each depositor treating the loan money as an asset on the books. In this way, fractional reserves create new money, pyramiding it on top of a fraction of old deposits. Depending on reserve ratios and banking practices, an initial deposit of $1,000, thanks to this "money multiplier," turns into deposits of $10,000.[2] The Fed depends heavily on this system of fractional reserves, using the banking system as the engine through which new money is

2. This process is well described in Murray N. Rothbard, *The Mystery of Banking* (Auburn, AL: Mises Institute, 2008, 1983). It is even described, with a different spin, on the Federal Reserve's own Web site.

injected into the economy as a whole. It adds reserves to the balances of member banks in the hope of inspiring ever more lending.

From the depositor point of view, this system has created certain illusions. As customers of the bank, we tend to believe that we can have both perfect security for our money, drawing on it whenever we want and never expecting it not to be there, while still earning a regular rate of return on that same money. In a true free market, however, there tends to be a tradeoff: you can enjoy the service of a money warehouse or you can loan your money to the bank and hope for a return on your investment. You can't usually have both. The Fed, however, by backing up this fractional-reserve system with a promise of endless bailouts and money creation, attempts to keep the illusion going.

Even with a government-guaranteed system of fractional reserves, the system is always vulnerable to collapse at the right moments, namely, when all depositors come asking for their money in the course of a run (think of the scene in *It's a Wonderful Life*). The whole history of modern banking legislation and reform can be seen as an elaborate attempt to patch the holes in this leaking boat. Thus have we created deposit insurance, established the "too big to fail" doctrine, created schemes for emergency injections, and all the rest, so as to keep afloat a system that is inherently unstable.

What I've described is a telescoped version of several hundreds of developments, but it accurately explains the continued drive to push forward with money that is infinitely elastic and with banking institutions that are guaranteed through government legislation not to fail, that is, central banking as we know it. Just so that we are clear: the modern system of money and banking is not a free-market system. It is a system that is half socialized—propped up by government—and one that could never be sustained as it is in a clean market environment. And this is the core of the problem.

In examining the history of the Fed in particular, we must start far back in the story, since fractional-reserve banking had already become part of established banking practices in the nineteenth century, a fact that goes a very long way to explain the source of periodic instability.

The story can be said to begin in 1775, when the Continental Congress issued a paper money called the continental, as in "not worth a continental." The currency was inflated to the point of disaster, and price controls didn't come close to working to stop it. This was the first great hyperinflation in U.S. history, and it gave rise to a hard-money school of thought that would agitate against central banking and paper money for many generations since. It also explains why the Constitution placed a ban on paper money and permitted only gold and silver as money.

In 1791, the First Bank of the United States was chartered, and in 1792, Congress passed the Coinage Act recognizing the dollar as the national currency, the original of which dates back to the 1400s with the German coin, the thaler. Fortunately, the charter of the incipient central bank was not renewed and it expired in 1811.

In 1812, with war raging between Britain and the United States, the government issued notes to finance the conflict, resulting in suspensions of payment as well as inflation. Inflation during wartime is something you might expect, but instead of permitting normal conditions to return, Congress chartered the Second Bank of the United States in 1816. The bank aided and abetted ever more expansion and the creation of a boom-bust cycle.

The nineteenth-century American banking theorist Condy Raguet explains:[3]

Those who can remember the events of that period will not have forgotten the abuse of the public forbearance exhibited by them upon that occasion. The sanction of the community was extended to them during the continuance of the war then existing with Great Britain, on account of the belief that their condition was forced upon them by the peculiar circumstances of the country; but no sooner had peace returned in the early part of 1815, than all their pledges were violated, and instead of manifesting by their actions a desire to contract their loans so as to place themselves in a situation for complying with their obligations, they actually expanded the currency by extraordinary issues, whilst there was no existing check upon them, until its depreciation became so great that speculation and overtrading in all their disastrous forms, involved the country in a scene of wretchedness, from which it did not recover in ten years.

Finally, the inevitable downturn occurred with the Panic of 1819. This panic ended peacefully precisely because nothing

3. Condy Raguet, *A Treatise on Currency and Banking* (New York: Kelley Reprints, 1967, 1840), p. 156.

was done to stop it. Jefferson pointed out that, in any case, the panic was only wiping out wealth that was entirely fictitious to begin with. Today this panic is but a footnote in the history books.[4] After massive political agitation, and following Andrew Jackson's executive order that withdrew the federal government's deposits from the bank, the Second Bank was also allowed to be closed in 1836.

The war between North and South set off another round of inflationary finance, however, eventually killing off wartime currencies and prompting another deflation after the war. This set the stage for a gold standard to be established that was solid but not perfect. It was the existence of flaws—banks were permitted fractional reserves and were beginning to rely on more and more regulations to dampen competition—that created the dynamic that led to the Federal Reserve.

The ostensible impetus for the creation of the Federal Reserve was the banking panic of 1907, but the drive, as mentioned, began long before. Jacob Schiff, head of Kuhn, Loeb, & Co., gave a speech in 1906 that actually began the push for a European-style central bank. He explained that the "country needed money to prevent the next crisis." He worked with his partner Paul Moritz Warburg and Frank A. Vanderlip of the National City Bank of New York to create a new commission that would deliver a report to the New York Chamber of Commerce in 1906. It called for a "central bank of issue under the control of the government." They began to work within other organizations to push the agenda, winning over the

4. Murray N. Rothbard, *The Panic of 1819* (Auburn, AL: Mises Institute, 2008).

American Banking Association and many important players in government.[5]

Once the groundwork was laid, the crisis atmosphere of 1907 assisted greatly in creating the conditions that led to the founding of the Fed. It was a brief contraction, but during it many banks suspended specie payments, that is, they stopped paying out gold to depositors until the crisis passed. This led to a consolidation of opinion in favor of a general guarantor of all deposits.

A point we learn from this event and every other banking panic in U.S. history is that crises have always led to greater centralization. A system that is mixed between freedom and the state is a shaky system, and its internal contradictions have been resolved not by tending toward a free market but rather through a trend toward statism. It is not surprising, then, that academic opinion swung in favor of central banking, too, with most important economists—having long forgotten their classical roots—seeing new magic powers associated with elastic money.

In 1908, Congress created a National Monetary Commission to look into the general idea of banking reform. The commission was staffed mostly by people close to the largest banks: First National Bank of New York, Kuhn, Loeb, Bankers Trust Company, and the Continental National Bank of

5. The details of the founding of the Fed are reported in William Greider, *Secrets of the Temple* (New York: Simon & Schuster, 1987), pp. 276–289; Murray N. Rothbard, *A History of Money and Banking in the United States: The Colonial Era to World War II* (Auburn, AL: Mises Institute, 2002), pp. 162–183; and James Livingston, *Origins of the Federal Reserve System: Money, Class, and Corporate Capitalism, 1890–1913* (Ithaca, NY: Cornell University Press, 1986).

Chicago. The NMC traveled around Europe and returned to the United States to continue the propaganda.

By 1909, President William Howard Taft had already endorsed a central bank, while the *Wall Street Journal* ran a fourteen-part series on the need for a central bank. The unsigned series was written by an NMC member, Charles A. Conant, who was the commission's chief public relations man. The series made all the usual arguments for elasticity but added several additional functions that the central bank could play, including manipulating the discount rate and gold flows as well as actively bailing out failing banks. What followed was a series of public speeches, pamphleteering, scholarly statements, political speeches, and press releases by merchant groups.

By November 1910, the time was right for drafting the bill that would become the Federal Reserve Act. A secret meeting was convened at the coastal Georgia resort called the Jekyll Island Club, co-owned by J. P. Morgan himself. The press said it was a duck-hunting expedition. Those who attended took elaborate steps to preserve their secrecy, but history recorded precisely who was there: John D. Rockefeller's man in the senate, Nelson Aldrich, Morgan senior partner Henry Davison, German émigré and central banking advocate Paul Warburg, National City Bank vice president Frank Vanderlip, and NMC staffer A. Piatt Andrew, who was also Assistant Secretary of the Treasury to President Taft.

So we had two Rockefellers, two Morgans, one Kuhn, Loeb person, and one economist. In this group, we find the essence of the Fed: powerful bankers with powerful government officials working together to have the nation's money system serve their interests, justified by economists there to provide the scientific gloss. It has been pretty much the same ever since.

They worked in secrecy for a full week. The structure of the Federal Reserve was proposed at this meeting. It was not to be a European-style central bank—or rather, it would be, but the structure would be different. It would be "decentralized" into twelve member banks, providing something of a cover for the cartelization that was actually taking place. The full plan was presented to the National Monetary Commission in 1911. Then the propaganda was really stepped up, with newspaper editorials, phony citizens' leagues, and endorsements from trade organizations. The next step was to remove the Republican partisanship from the bill and replace it with a bipartisan appearance, and the bill passed.

The essence of the Federal Reserve Act was largely unchanged from when it was first hatched years earlier. With a vote by Congress, the government would confer legal legitimacy on a cartel of the largest bankers and permit them to inflate the money supply at will, providing for themselves and the financial system liquidity in times of need, while insulating themselves against the consequences of bad loans and overextension of credit.

Hans Sennholz has called the creation of the Fed "the most tragic blunder ever committed by Congress. The day it was passed, old America died and a new era began. A new institution was born that was to cause, or greatly contribute to, the unprecedented economic instability in the decades to come."[6]

6. Hans F. Sennholz, *Money and Freedom* (Grove City, PA: Libertarian Press), p. 21.

It was a form of financial socialism that benefited the rich and the powerful. As for the excuse, it was then what it is now. The claim is that the Fed would protect the monetary and financial system against inflation and violent swings in market activity. It would stabilize the system by providing stimulus when it was necessary and pulling back on inflation when the economy became overheated.

A statement by the Comptroller of the Currency in 1914 promised that a ridiculous nirvana would be ushered in by the Fed. It "supplies a circulating medium absolutely safe," the statement said. Further, "under the operation of this law such financial and commercial crises, or 'panics,' as this country experienced in 1873, in 1893, and again in 1907, with the attendant misfortunes and prostrations, seem to be mathematically impossible."[7]

And here is another remarkable promise from the Comptroller of the Currency:[8]

Under the provisions of the new law the failure of efficiently and honestly managed banks is practically impossible and a closer watch can be kept on member banks. Opportunities for a more thorough and complete examination are furnished for each particular bank. These facts should reduce the dangers from dishonest and incompetent management to a minimum. It is hoped that the national-bank failures can hereafter be virtually eliminated.

7. Elgin Groseclose, *America's Money Machine: The Story of the Federal Reserve* (Westport, CT: Arlington House, 1966), p. 85.

8. Ibid., p. 86.

Purchasing Power of the U.S. Dollar, January 1913 = $1.00

In practice the reality has been much different. One only needs to reflect on the dramatic decline in the value of the dollar that has taken place since the Fed was established in 1913. The goods and services you could buy for $1.00 in 1913 now cost nearly $21.00. Another way to look at this is from the perspective of the purchasing power of the dollar itself. It has fallen to less than $0.05 of its 1913 value. We might say that the government and its banking cartel have together stolen $0.95 of every dollar as they have pursued a relentlessly inflationary policy.[9]

The same is true of other currencies controlled by a central bank. It is not, however, true of gold. Here is a general overview, courtesy of the American Institute for Economic Research:[10]

9. Data from the Federal Reserve Bank of St. Louis.

10. The chart can be viewed online at http://www.aier.org/images/stories/research/ch_p5.pdf.

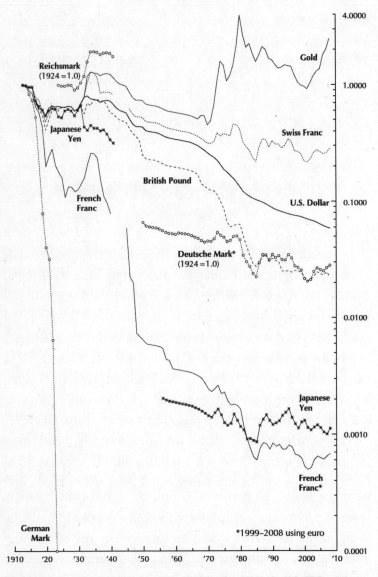

**Purchasing Power in the United States of Gold and Selected Currencies
(1913 = 1.0)**

Note: Purchasing power calculated from the implicit price deflator for U.S. GDP and the exchange rates of foreign currencies for U.S. dollars.

As for business cycles and the abolition of panics, the data show otherwise. Recessions of the twentieth century as documented by the National Bureau of Economic Research include: 1918–1919, 1920–1921, 1923–1924, 1926–1927, 1929–1933, 1937–1938, 1945, 1948–1949, 1953–1954, 1957–1958, 1960–1961, 1969–1970, 1973–1975, 1980, 1981–1982, 1990–1991, 2001, and 2007, which is the current panic of which there is no end in sight.

Some mathematical impossibility!

The one aspect of the great promise that has been kept, not entirely but generally, is the promise that banks will not fail in the way they used to. But consider whether this is really a good thing. What if we had a law against business failure? It raises an obvious question: if businesses are not allowed to fail, what guarantee is in place that will give them incentive to succeed with soundness and productivity to the common good? In a capitalist economy, the prospect of failure imposes discipline and consumer service. It is an essential aspect of the competitive marketplace, whereas a promise against failure only entrenches inefficiency and incompetency.

In other words, bank failures are no more to be regretted than any other business failures. They are a normal feature of the free enterprise system. What about depositors? In a competitive and free system, deposits would not be unsafe; any that were not paid back that were promised would fall under the laws of protection against fraud. Unsafe deposits would be loans to the bank that would be treated like any other risky investment. Consumers would keep a more careful watch over the institutions that are handling their money and stop trusting regulators in Washington, who in fact have not done a good job in ferreting out incompetence.

But this is not the place to explain the workings of a free-market banking system. I raise the point only to underscore the broader lesson that no firm in a free market should enjoy absolute protection against failure. A continued process of trial and error is the way that institutions achieve the goal of efficiency and soundness. Consider the Soviet case: to my knowledge, no business ever went under in the Soviet system, but society in general grew ever poorer. Think of that Soviet system applied to the banking industry and you have the Fed.

Understanding this history of the Fed's founding and effects helps take some of the mystery out of it. Some people claim that the Fed is nothing but a private corporation that is working to enrich itself at our expense. Other people claim that it is a government operation that works to provide funds for the government when it can no longer get away with taxing us.

Neither opinion is precisely correct. Actually, the Fed is a public-private partnership, a coalition of large banks that are the owners working with the blessing of the government, which appoints its managers. In some way, it is the worst of both the corporate and the government worlds, with each side providing a contribution to an institution that has been horribly detrimental to American prosperity.

In any case, William Greider is exactly correct that the advent of the Fed represented "the beginning of the end of laissez-faire."[11] It turned the entire money system over to public management on behalf of political causes.

---

11. William Greider, *Secrets of the Temple*, p. 280.

Over the years, the Fed has been granted ever more leeway in the means it uses to inflate the money supply. It can now buy just about anything it wants and write it down as an asset. When it buys debt, it buys with newly created money. It maintains a strict system of low-reserve ratios that allows banks to pile loans on top of deposits and take the new deposits as the basis for ever more loans. It can set the federal funds rate at a level to its liking and influence interest across the entire economy. It intervenes in currency markets and other markets.

There have been many consequences of the Fed that were unforeseen even by its architects. They might have imagined that the Fed would indeed help smooth out the business cycle, provided you think of the real problem of the cycle as its bust phase when credit contracts. The Fed can indeed provide liquidity in these times by a simple operation of printing more paper money to cover deposits. But if you think of the cycle as beginning in the boom phase—when money and credit are loose and lending soars to fund unsustainable projects—matters change substantially.

In 1912, Ludwig von Mises wrote a book called *The Theory of Money and Credit*[12] that was widely acclaimed all over Europe. In it he warned that the creation of central banks would worsen and spread business cycles rather than eliminate them. It works as follows. The central bank on a whim can reduce the interest rate that it charges member banks for loans. It can buy government debt and add that debt as an asset on its balance

12. Ludwig von Mises, *The Theory of Money and Credit* (New Haven, CT: Yale University Press, 1953).

sheet. It can reduce the reserve coverage for loans at member banks. But in doing all of this, it is toying with the signals that the banking industry is sending to borrowers. Businesses are fooled into taking out longer-term loans and starting projects that cannot be sustained. Investors flush with new cash put the money in stocks or buy homes, activities that spread a kind of buying-and-selling fever among the general population.

The problem is that all of this activity creates an illusory prosperity, a false boom. When lower interest rates result from real saving, the banking system is signaling that the necessary sacrifice of present consumption has taken place in order to fund long-term investment. But when central banks push down rates on a whim, the impression is created that the savings are there when they are in fact completely absent. The resulting bust becomes inevitable as goods that come to production can't be purchased, and reality sets in by waves. Businesses fail, homes are foreclosed upon, and people bail out of stocks or whatever is the fashionable investment of the day.

That phony money creates a false boom is not an unknown fact in history. Thomas Paine observed in the late eighteenth century that paper money threatened to turn the country into a nation of "stockjobbers." In fact, this can even happen when the money is not paper. The famous case of tulip mania in the Dutch golden era was driven by gold inflows from around Europe after the government gave a massive coinage subsidy to all comers.[13]

---

13. Doug French, *Early Speculative Bubbles and Increases in the Supply of Money* (Auburn, AL: Mises Institute, 2009).

International markets complicate the picture by allowing the boom phase of the cycle to continue longer than it otherwise would, as foreigners buy up and hold new debt, using it as collateral for their own monetary extensions. But eventually they, too, become ensnared in the boom-bust cycle of false prosperity followed by an all-too-real bust. International markets can delay but not finally eliminate the inevitable results of monetary expansion.

Now, knowledge of this problem was not well spread among bankers and government officials in 1913 when the Fed was created. But it wouldn't be long until it would become apparent that the Fed would bring not stability but more instability, not shorter booms and busts but deeper and longer ones. The longest one of all, dramatically exacerbated by bad economic policy, was the Great Depression.

We might be entering into another phase of extreme crisis.

CHAPTER 3

MY INTELLECTUAL INFLUENCES

My interest in monetary economics began quite early. Born in 1935, I remember the tail end of the Depression and the shortages of World War II. Being from a family that taught hard work, frugality, and savings as virtues, I knew early on that even a few pennies were not to be ignored. But then again, a copper penny actually had real value.

I recall walking with my brothers to a local store to buy candy. We each had four or five pennies and got a small bag full of candy for them. Today, we not only can't afford to make our pennies out of copper, we can't even afford to make them out of zinc. The penny is destined to be made of steel or eliminated as a cost-savings measure. Indeed, the penny is a nuisance for most of us today.

My first job, and that of my brothers, was to assist my dad in a small dairy run out of our basement. Even at the age of five, the incentive system was instilled in me. Our job was to make sure all the glass bottles, which had been hand washed, were clean. It was bad for business if a customer saw a black spot in the bottom of a milk bottle. For each dirty bottle we found as we removed them from the conveyer belt and placed them into a wooden case, we were rewarded a penny. It didn't take long for us to know when a certain uncle was washing the bottles, since more dirty bottles were found on those days.

This experience taught me the importance of working, and the value of a penny. My parents did not believe in allowances, but I was a natural saver, even in my early years. It seems at times that being a saver or a spender is an innate tendency, and early habits are retained throughout life. My early experience of learning the value of a penny served me well when it came time to pay for my education.

My dad had two concerns about the milk itself. First, he tested for quality by tasting each can of milk coming in from any of numerous farmers; he could tell if the cows had gotten into an onion patch, for example, which ruined the milk. The other was a concern that the milk that might have been diluted by water. In time I realized that the crime of dilution was identical to the crime of managing an elastic currency by the dilution principle.

My dad was not a coin collector, but he did understand the value of hard work, savings, and even a penny. Somewhere along the way, out of fascination with the switch from the Indian Head penny to the Lincoln Head penny, he started throwing Indian Heads into a coffee can—pennies that I'm sure came from our retail milk sales. At the time, a quart of milk cost 15 cents.

I'm not sure of my exact age, but I probably became interested in coin collecting during World War II. I had access to the coins that came in through milk sales, and early on as a newspaper boy for the *Pittsburgh Press*. That can of Indian

Heads sat on a desk in our kitchen for years. By the 1940s, the Indian Head penny had long since left circulation. There were 986 pennies in the can as I recall. I would scan them and sort them, and I knew exactly which pennies were there.

Although it was obvious that I was the most interested of the five brothers in coin collecting, there was no way that those pennies would become mine because of the fairness doctrine of our parents—"no special favors."

I saved my money, and when I had $20, I negotiated a deal with my dad: $20 for 986 pennies. It was a big transaction for me, but only I knew that buried in that can was a 1909-S in good condition, which even then made the purchase a great deal. I still have that particular penny and most of the other 985.

Pennies are a nuisance for most of us today. But that special 1909-S has kept up with inflation and more due to its numismatic value. As a young boy, I understood how rarity and quality in a coin gave it value—the fundamentals of numismatics. There were only 309,000 1909-S pennies minted. It was years before I understood the relationship between the money supply and the value of our currency and the business cycle, but even back then I was impressed with the relationship of low mintage and value.

During World War II, I heard the radio announcements urging us all to buy war bonds. We were encouraged at school to do the same, and I'm sure newspapers encouraged their purchase. It was the patriotic thing to do. I did it; my whole family did it as well. We would save $18.75 to buy a $25 war bond that matured in ten years, earning 2.9 percent interest.

It was only a stunt, as I found out many years later. Almost all the funding for the war came from taxes and the Fed's inflating of the currency. The Buy Bonds campaign was a psychological tool to keep everyone focused on the war. Wage and price controls and rationing made a bad situation worse, yet it was our duty to march in lockstep with all the mandates and controls.

From personal memory and historic records, I know the Depression was not ended by the beginning of the war, as many still claim. War's mass death and property confiscation and destruction are never a benefit to the economy, yet the warning that bad economic times frequently lead to war—when a country can least afford it—is appropriate for today. War distracts from economic problems, a benefit to bad politicians. Unemployment rates go down when millions are engaged in the war effort, even forced into it. All too often these politically convenient wars are not at all necessary.

I recall as an eight- or nine-year-old wondering about all this while collecting coins, buying stamps, putting them in a book, then buying a bond and thinking it was a bit cumbersome. Why didn't they just print what they needed? I sought an answer from my oldest brother. Not realizing that's exactly what they were doing, my brother logically explained to me why that wouldn't work. He simply said, "If they did that, the money wouldn't be worth anything." That may be way oversimplified, yet it was true.

That short conversation stayed with me over the years as I tried to understand the process of currency inflation and how prices are subjectively established. Although the monetary system may be a crucial factor in itself, it is not the sole deciding factor in setting the prices of goods and services. It's a bit more complicated than that. It was only after the war and after price controls were removed, with a significant increase in the money supply, that more people knew what was going on. Prices escalated sharply between 1945 and 1947, at an annualized rate of 17 percent.

I have memories of rationing during World War II. Ration stamps were required for crucial items like gasoline, butter, and meat. When we sold a pound of butter at our house, we had to also collect the ration stamps. These conditions existed along with wage and price controls—hardly a good lesson for young Americans trying to learn what freedom was! Without the designated rationing stamps passed out by the government, these selected goods were not available, unless they were bought in the underground (free) market. Prohibition or rationing was so detrimental that other markets quickly developed out of need.

I'm sure some believed that rationing scarce resources during the war was absolutely necessary. Others were quite aware that it was part of the war propaganda to keep people focused on the political goal. Those who understood the free market knew that during a crisis or time of shortage, the market is required more than ever.

In allocating scarce resources, imposing wage and price controls is the last thing we need government to do.[1] It only exacerbates the problem, as I well remember. We really never learn much from our mistakes. Wage and price controls were used again during the Korean War and in the early 1970s,

---

1. Robert Schuettinger and Eamonn Butler, *Forty Centuries of Wage and Price Controls* (Washington, DC: Heritage Foundation, 1979; Auburn, AL: Mises Institute, 2009).

after the breakdown of the Bretton Woods Agreement, the unstable gold-exchange standard system established in haste after World War II.

I remember my dad as being straitlaced. He believed that we should all follow the rules and obey the government. Yet I do remember being with him on Saturday afternoons when a butcher shop in town had all the meat you wanted, at a price—and without ration stamps. Evidently, it was worth bending the rules a bit to get some meat on the table for his family. There seemed to be no secret about what was going on. Business was brisk, and the event took place across the street from the police station. This was probably my first real-life experience in the free market solving problems generated by government mischief.

Sadly, we haven't learned a whole lot. Even today, as we're struggling to get out of a gigantic economic crisis, the principle of government meddling in pricing goods and services persists. The worse the crisis gets, the more government interferes in the pricing mechanism. Today the black market in labor and goods is huge.

Our disastrous tax code has contributed substantially to the need for the underground economy. This need will surely grow as the economy further deteriorates. In economic terms, all this activity is beneficial in the underground, despite politicians' cries that the government is being cheated out of hundreds of billions of dollars in tax revenue. If the market quits functioning, the underground economy will expand exponentially. In some other countries the underground market is responsible for keeping the economy afloat.

After World War II, economic conditions improved. My

grandparents lived nearby and had some land that they were contemplating selling. I recall my dad urging my grandmother to sell the land, but she was hesitant. She was concerned about the money. My grandfather was born in Germany and came to the United States at the age of fourteen and settled in Pittsburgh. My grandmother was born in the United States, but her parents were both immigrants from Germany. In 1926 they sailed to Germany to visit relatives. I'm sure they heard stories about the German inflation of the 1920s, and this influenced her thinking.

I remember the answer my grandmother gave my dad. She thought she should not sell and should hold on to the land "in case the money goes bad." Although the U.S. inflation after World War II was mild compared to the German inflation of 1923, it must have been a concern for her.

Shortly after the war, wage and price controls were removed and consumer prices advanced sharply, which also must have contributed to her concern. Retail prices were rising as a consequence of the inflation to finance the war.

My grandmother was devout and knew the Bible. She had read Genesis 47:15: "So when the money failed in the land of Egypt and in the land of Canaan, all the Egyptians came to Joseph and said, 'Give us bread, for why should we die in your presence? For the money has failed.'"

Our current problem was well established, even in ancient Egypt. Debased currencies fail. Governments cannot manage money.

Although the destruction of the dollar has been slow and insidious, deep concern existed even before President Nixon, in 1971, eliminated what remained of the gold standard. During the Korean War, inflation was a serious enough concern, just as it had been during the 1970s, to disguise it with wage and price controls.

Today's politicians in Washington, oblivious as usual to the dangers of inflation, show no concern for the dollar or the operations of the Federal Reserve. They are, instead, terrified of deflation. Think of what the word *deflation* means. Defined as a declining money stock, deflation can actually be economically clarifying. It causes banks to tighten up their lending standards and encourages businesses to run tighter operations. It can put the squeeze on government, as it becomes more costly to service the debt. None of these is a regrettable trend.

Another definition of deflation concerns a falling price level. This is another way of saying that your money becomes more valuable over time. That is not something to regret, either. Business can operate and thrive under these conditions: look at the software and computer industries since the 1980s. And if we look back at the last quarter of the nineteenth century, increased purchasing power (*deflation*) was accompanied by the greatest period of economic growth in world history, with the benefits of capitalism spreading to all sectors of society.

So I do not believe deflation is a threat. In fact, we would be lucky to face such a "threat"! The real threat we face is the opposite. The concern my grandmother expressed may have been overblown and early, but we as a nation are setting the stage for "the money going bad," German-style. We may be getting closer to that day than anybody realizes.

The janitor at our grade school in Greentree, Pennsylvania, was an interesting character. He was seen as a bit of an old sage, at least by me. Others who attended that school will remember

Willy (William Foley). He was chief cook and bottle washer for the entire building—no assistants. That is, except in the summer months when a few of us got jobs scrubbing walls and windows and painting. We were all of twelve or thirteen years old, and I'm sure child labor laws were never on anyone's mind. Our early wages were surely less than a dollar, since at that time I also worked in a drugstore for 35 cents an hour. My experience in the drugstore paid off surprisingly well by the time I got to college and secured the manager's job at the Bullet Hole, the coffee hangout for students at Gettysburg College.

The experience working for Willy and listening to his philosophizing was stimulating. In a way, he probably taught me as much about life as any of my teachers. He could easily be a candidate for the most unforgettable character I have ever met.

He talked about life struggles, but he also acted as a policeman of sorts. Though a "mere" janitor, he had some discipline authority, or at least bad behavior could easily be reported to higher authorities. But that's where he excelled, cautioning us, advising us, and mostly protecting us from stern discipline if certain events were to become known to the principal. The principal was a World War I veteran whose voice reflected exposure to poison gas in the fighting. He also believed in harsh corporal punishment. So most of us saw Willy as a trusted friend.

I recall one subject on which Willy did a bit of ranting. The "bankers" were the source of our problems, and I heard the charge more than once. I had no idea what he was talking about, and for years afterward wondered about it. Unfortunately, I didn't know enough to quiz him. But as the years went by, I surmised a few things.

Willy was old when he came to our school—it was a retirement job for him. He told stories of once being a glass blower and indicated that it was a high-paying job and allowed him to buy a fancy horse-drawn rig. Obviously, this was before automobiles.

In thinking back, I decided he may well have been old enough to vote in 1896. Maybe he was influenced by William Jennings Bryan's populism and attacks on bankers. After many years, because I never forgot the charge that the bankers caused all our economic and political problems, I decided he was a product of the Populist-Progressive Era of the late 1800s and the early 1900s.

Although William Jennings Bryan was hardly a champion of our cause, he was a fan of Andrew Jackson's and early on was an enemy of central banking. In his "Cross of Gold" speech, Bryan shouted: "What we need is *our* Andrew Jackson to stand, as Jackson stood, against the encroachments of organized wealth!" Bryan credited Jackson with having destroyed "the bank conspiracy and saved America."

Bryan was no libertarian, but his attack on powerful banking interests should make us aware of the historical precedent for protests against these elites. Today's building coalition that is attacking current central banking operations might even be more radical; it is certainly more educated.

So far, the leadership of the Republicans and the Democrats has resisted any attack on the Federal Reserve, but that will probably change as blame for our current financial crisis can and should be laid squarely at the feet of the Fed. The money issue is once again becoming a key political issue.

In an Economics 101 class at Gettysburg College, a bit of a revelation hit me when I discovered that most money was not money at all, but rather money substitutes. The economy thrives, I was told, on all of us circulating checkbook paper credits kept on a log at the bank. In my sheltered life, I thought we worked for money, paid our bills in money, and when we had too much on hand, we saved it in a bank and it earned interest. That's what I did with my pennies and quarters earned from lawn mowing and delivering papers and milk.

But now, it was explained to me, the bank only had to have a fraction of the actual money on hand. I was told this facilitated economic growth through the concept of fractional-reserve banking. It made me question, but surely not enough, the system the professor was now explaining to me. In a way, it seemed to be a pretty neat trick.

My first reaction might have been something like Paul Begala's startling discovery, while serving in the Clinton administration, regarding executive orders: "Stroke of the pen, law of the land, kinda cool." Begala, of course, was ecstatic over the remarkable shortcut for passing laws by keeping Congress from interfering with the legislative process. That's how those who benefit from inflation must feel about the Federal Reserve System—"kinda cool."

The banks certainly enjoy the benefits of the current monetary system and the principle of fractional-reserve banking. Just like Begala, the recipients of the benefits that come from the fraudulent system of money are pleased with a shortcut to acquiring that money. Even after their scheme to enrich themselves falls apart, as it inevitably does, their expectations remain the same. They claim they provide an invaluable public service and deserve continued support from the public treasury. But this time it is happening more directly, through direct taxpayer-supported bailouts. Once this principle is established, the line grows longer and nearly everyone demands assistance.

The seeds of financial distrust were sown decades ago, as I discovered in a college class in the 1950s. The corrupt system lasted a long time, but now payback is upon us.

In the 1960s, I discovered the writings of economists such as Ludwig von Mises, F. A. Hayek, Murray N. Rothbard, and Hans F. Sennholz. I gradually found the answers I had been searching for. Even for the experts, it literally took centuries to fully understand the nature of money and the business cycle. Unfortunately, those in charge of our government and banking system are still denying the truth regarding money that was discovered many decades ago.

While I was serving in the U.S. Air Force and stationed at Kelly Air Force Base as a flight surgeon, my next-door neighbor, a fellow physician, taught me something practical about the system. He understood hard money and was also influenced by his Mormon faith, which taught him self-reliance and frugality. I found out that on a regular basis he was sending off and buying uncirculated silver dollars. At the time, silver was still under $1.21 an ounce, and therefore the incentive to buy and melt silver dollars for their silver content did not exist. But he did, however, pay a premium over the normal value. Although the added cost was very small, it seemed a little strange to me that somebody would pay $1.05 for a silver dollar that could be obtained at the bank for $1.00 for routine purchases. The 5 percent extra was the cost for getting an uncirculated coin.

My friend's instincts were right about stocking up on silver dollars. It was not too many years later, in 1965, that silver was removed from the coinage. Even LBJ's claim that he would mint so many Kennedy half-dollars that the market would become saturated and force the coins to stay in circulation was wrong. He didn't understand Gresham's law (that money overvalued by the government will drive out money that is undervalued by the government), and the more he minted, which turned out to be a record number, the faster they were removed from circulation. Since silver never dropped below $1.21 an ounce, the Kennedy silver half-dollar never circulated to any degree.

Another physician I knew during this time would periodically travel to Las Vegas and bring home a bag of silver dollars. These he got at face value. Silver dollars at the time were still being used in casino slot machines. Wouldn't that be fascinating, to watch and listen to real silver dollars being used? Credit cards, dollar bills, and tokens—how boring! And I don't even gamble.

The monetary event that prompted me to enter politics occurred on August 15, 1971. That Sunday evening, Richard "We are all Keynesians now" Nixon announced the U.S. government would default on its pledge to deliver gold to any foreign government holding U.S. dollars at the rate of one ounce of gold for each $35.

In addition, wage and price controls were put in place, along with a 10 percent import tariff. Instead of the markets collapsing, as I thought they should, the move was immediately praised by the Chamber of Commerce, and the stock market soared. The problems came a little bit later and lasted for a decade. The stock market rally quickly fizzled.

This was the third broken promise by our government regarding gold backing to our dollar. Lincoln did it in the Civil War, and FDR did it in 1933 when he confiscated gold from the American people and made it illegal for American citizens to own gold. Roosevelt took the gold at $20 an ounce and promptly revalued it at $35. The citizens lost, the government profited.

Profits from this process were used to initially fund the Exchange Stabilization Fund, which is still in operation today. It is a slush fund hidden from the scrutiny of the Congress and has already used $50 billion in the current bailout process. It is a self-funding operation, earning enough interest from the Treasury to do at will what they want. Under the law, it is still permitted to meddle in the gold market, which I suspect it does.

Tragically, the courts supported this illegal theft by Roosevelt from the people and ruled that all private and government promises to pay bondholders in gold were null and void. So much for Article 1, Section 10, which places responsibility on the federal government to protect contracts, not to deliberately break them.

August 15, 1971, was a major event in the history of the American dollar. In many ways, it was saying the U.S. government was insolvent—it could not meet its monetary commitments. The worldwide run on the American system arrived and the United States refused to pay. A fiat dollar reserve standard replaced the Bretton Woods pseudo-gold standard. There was nothing unexpected here. The failure of Bretton Woods was predicted early on by the Austrian economists, especially Henry Hazlitt, who was writing daily articles for the editorial page of the *New York Times*.[2] Austrian school economists also knew, even in 1971, that the new paper standard would not provide stability to the financial system.

The shift to a new monetary regime was an unprecedented experiment in global monetary planning, a wholesale plunge into the world of paper currency. With no backing for the dollar at all, Americans became completely reliant on the Federal Reserve to manage our money and to do so without any outside discipline.

The chaos was dramatic. The dollar was sharply devalued, and price inflation became a major problem in the decade of the 1970s, as did steadily rising interest rates. But what impressed me most was that the Austrian economists who made predictions a long time ago were proven correct.

It was the consequences of this event in 1971 that prompted me to decide on a lark in late 1973 to run for Congress in 1974. Texas was still a Democratic state, and had only three Republicans in a delegation of twenty-four congressmen. The district I was running in had never been held by a Republican. In 1974, it remained a Democratic district.

My first victory didn't come until a special election in the spring of 1976. At the time, I was just anxious to have a forum in which to talk about monetary policy and its relationship to

2. Henry Hazlitt, *From Bretton Woods to World Inflation* (Washington, DC: Regnery, 1984; Auburn, AL: Mises Institute, 2009).

the inexorable growth of our federal government. I was as surprised as anyone that this effort to spread a message about monetary policy and freedom would lead to a career of sorts in politics.

I was convinced that if one did not play the role of Santa Claus or errand boy for a district, it would be impossible to win a seat in the U.S. Congress. My wife, Carol, warned me at the time that running for Congress could be dangerous: "You could end up winning." I dismissed her concern and didn't anticipate that I had a chance. I was pleasantly surprised.

As significant as the events of the 1970s were, the financial chaos we are now witnessing is much more significant. The fact that the system was held together for longer than many Austrian economists expected only means that the financial bubble, the debt, the malinvestment, and the international imbalances would become that much greater.

The market made every effort to correct monetary mistakes of these past thirty-seven years. The Federal Reserve was able to minimize the corrections only to guarantee the current BIG ONE down the road. That, of course, means worldwide depression worse than the 1930s, unless we wake up rather quickly.

Dangerous times are indeed with us, and we will be forced to devise a new monetary system just as we were required to do at the end of the Bretton Woods system. But there is no looking back, no return to the old 1944 agreement. Today, there's still wishful thinking, but the fiat dollar reserve standard that the world has blindly accepted for more than three decades is dying and the financial structure is disintegrating. What we decide to do now will affect the well-being of

American citizens for decades to come. There's no returning to the fiat dollar standard that evolved after August 15, 1971.

The 1970s were hectic, and establishment economists were mystified by a stagnant economy and rampant price inflation, prompting a new term to describe the conditions: *stagflation*.

Being in Congress in the late 1970s and early 1980s and serving on the House Banking Committee, I met and got to question several Federal Reserve Board chairmen: Arthur Burns, William G. Miller, and Paul Volcker.

Of the three, I had the most interaction with Volcker. He was more personable and smarter than the others, including the more recent board chairmen Alan Greenspan and Ben Bernanke. In my second tour of congressional duty starting in 1997, I had the opportunity to quiz them.

In 1980, a major piece of banking legislation, the Monetary Control Act, was passed; many considered it a prelude to the savings and loan crisis in that decade. I expressed my concern to Chairman Volcker at a hearing that reserve requirements could be lowered to zero and the Federal Reserve could buy any asset, including foreign debt.

Volcker invited me to a private breakfast to dissuade me from my interpretation. Lew Rockwell, my chief of staff, went with me to the breakfast. Interestingly, we arrived early and were talking with Volcker's aide when Volcker arrived. Before acknowledging Lew or me, he quickly went to his aide and asked, "What's the price of gold?"

At the time, the price of gold was soaring, and there was deep concern about inflation and the dollar's value on the international exchange markets. I believe central bankers are always looking at the price of gold, because they know what many of us know: in the long term, the best gauge for the soundness of a currency is the gold price.

The fallacy is that they believe if the gold price can be held in check, even artificially, it conveys confidence in the currency and the banking system. Defying market forces that want a higher price for gold by artificial means can only work temporarily. The market, or the *black market* if necessary, will always set the real prices of everything. Eventually, artificially fixing the price of gold will break down.

That's what happened in 1971. Dumping nearly 500 million ounces of gold at $35 an ounce in the 1960s never stopped the depreciation of the dollar. Still, central bankers were determined to keep a lid on the dollar price of gold. Volcker was called to the Fed to stop the inflation, and obviously he was intensely interested in the price of gold. The gold price was the crucial test for him, since by then the Fed had long given up on pretending it could "fix" the gold price forever. That effort, of course, was abandoned in 1971 with the closing of the gold window.

Volcker, as an assistant secretary of the Treasury in 1971, expressed great doubt about the wisdom of that particular move regarding gold. Casual conversation with Volcker as recently as 2008 confirmed these concerns, but he assured me that a gold standard was not the answer to today's problem.

The breakfast went well, and he was quite cordial. This is not something Greenspan ever invited me to do; nor do I expect an invitation anytime soon to a private breakfast and discussion with Bernanke. At the end of the breakfast, Volcker finally agreed that my interpretation of the language was correct, but assured me he would never lower reserve requirements to that degree or buy up worthless assets. His argument was that the Fed wanted this authority to have free rein in raising reserve requirements at will, as he indeed did with interest rates that broke the back of the raging inflation of the 1970s. As we were leaving, I said that, although I didn't expect that he would use these extreme powers, who knew if in the future we might just have someone who would. The future is now here.

The fact is that not only has this come to pass with Bernanke, but a great deal more authority has been usurped by the Fed, while Congress says little about it. The Fed today has ominous powers that Congress barely understands. There is essentially no oversight, no audit, and no control. And the Fed is protected by the Federal Reserve Act. That's why the Federal Reserve chairman has no obligation to answer questions that relate to Federal Open Market Committee meetings and actions taken in collusion with other central banks. Trillions of dollars can be created and injected into the economy with no obligation by the Fed to reveal who benefits. Lawsuits and freedom of information demands will not shake this information loose.

Arrogant is a mild word to describe the attitude of those who control our monetary system. When Bernanke was pressed to reveal further information about where the trillions of dollars were going from the Fed, the answer was quite clear: "We think that's counterproductive," that is, to reveal this information.[3]

My first exposure to the Austrian school of economics was through reading *The Road to Serfdom* by F. A. Hayek in the

---

3. "Bernanke Says Federal Reserve Won't Reveal Details on Loans," Bloomberg.com, November 18, 2008, story by Steve Matthews and Craig Torres.

early 1960s. Hayek, in the middle of the financial chaos following the breakdown of Bretton Woods, won the Nobel Prize in 1974 for his work on the economics of the business cycle. He is well known today for his work on competing currencies, developed in the market, along with the notion that a basket of currency may suffice as reserves. The basket of currency idea was something I never had a great affinity for, but I always accepted the idea that if it was developed by a nongovernment entity, no fraud involved, and it worked, so be it. It certainly would be superior to government fiat money.

Many years after reading *The Road to Serfdom*, I had the pleasure of hearing Hayek lecture in Washington, around 1980. Following that meeting, we had a private dinner together and spent several hours visiting. This dinner, which I remember well, further solidified my interest and confidence in Austrian economics.

Early on, I had heard Ludwig von Mises lecture at the University of Houston. This was probably in 1972, a year before his death. At that time I was extremely busy with my medical practice but saw a very small newspaper notice that Mises would be lecturing at the university on a weekday. I knew there was only one other physician in the town of Lake Jackson, Dr. Henry May, who would care about such an unusual event. I called him to see if he cared to travel the fifty miles to hear Mises. We rearranged our office schedules and made the trip.

Mises, at the time, was elderly but sharp. His subject was socialism, and his lecture explained why socialism always fails due to the absence of a free market pricing structure for capital goods. He was on his last lecture tour of the United States, and Houston may well have been his last stop. (Mises died on October 10, 1973, at ninety-two years of age.)

Not to our surprise, the university did not give him a prestigious reception. The lecture was held in a modest-sized classroom, but the place was overflowing. Popularizing Austrian economics at the time was in its very early stages, but it was obvious even then that there was a starvation for truth in economics. The early 1970s were truly hectic, and since gold prices were soaring and the dollar was dropping more and more, people were searching for solutions. Today, of course, the problems are so much worse and the need for answers even more urgent.

To say the least, my trip to Houston to hear Mises in person was an inspiration. I suspect that when the definitive history of the twentieth century is written, Mises will be considered one of the greatest economists, if not the greatest, of the century. That recognition won't come soon, because those in charge of the economic catastrophe are in total denial as to how they, who are now trying to rescue the system, caused all the problems we face. The universities are still cluttered, as is Washington, with Keynesians and socialists who refuse to give the slightest credibility to eliminating the central bank and instituting sound money. But this is changing, and fifty years from now, if we aren't driven into some dark age by our refusal to reassert the principles of liberty, the Austrian economists, and in particular Mises, will receive their due respect.

My interest in Austrian economics, and especially monetary policy, naturally directed my attention to the ongoing effort to legalize gold in America. Since Roosevelt's edict on

April 5, 1933, Americans were prohibited from owning gold. Only about three countries in the 1970s prohibited their citizens from owning gold, one being the Soviet Union.

Roosevelt, by executive order (6102) in 1933, confiscated all gold held by private citizens, with a few minor exceptions such as numismatic coins, and levied severe penalties on those who disobeyed. The penalty was $10,000 and/or ten years in prison. In today's money, that's more like $400,000. It was a rather bold, arrogant move from which much harm has come.

Today, as standard policy, Congress condones presidential executive orders, signing statements, judicial legislation, and agency regulations as all being permissible. Although it was a major event to confiscate gold, complaints were minimal. The crisis atmosphere and the need for the government to solve the economic crisis associated with the Depression squelched any complaints about the usurpation of power by FDR.

Since our crisis today may well evolve into something greater than what we suffered in the 1930s, we can only imagine, in this post 9/11 atmosphere, how much authority will be wielded by the executive branch. The only question is, will the American people resist, and if so, when?

At least the Roosevelt executive order was eventually reversed—not by a president who could have revoked the order, but finally by Congress responding to the pressure put on them by grassroots Americans. The system can work and did in January 1975, when Americans once again could own gold bullion coins.

Much credit has to be given to the late Jim Blanchard for his National Committee to Legalize Gold, which published a newsletter strictly to lobby for gold legalization.

Interestingly (and we were reminded of this during my presidential campaign), he had a biplane towing a banner over Nixon's 1973 inauguration parade saying "Legalize Gold." A freer America! Today that plane might be shot down. But it was President Ford who permitted once again ownership of gold. The authorities feared this move because the gold "price" is the ultimate test of value of a currency. Since the dumping of nearly 500 million ounces of gold in the 1960s didn't prevent the run on the dollar, the international authorities were determined to punish those "speculators" who were "hoarding" gold.

The gold price was bid up from $35 an ounce to $195 between 1971 and 1975, with the anticipation that the price would move even higher with American citizens coming into the market. Since the anticipated price increase was already discounted, traders were willing to sell, which they did, and gold went down precipitously from $195, and eventually to $102 by August 30, 1976. But it was more than just an adjustment by the traders. A concerted U.S. Treasury and IMF effort to knock the price down by dumping tons of gold onto the market served to put more pressure on the price decline. But obviously, it didn't last, and gold resumed its upward movement.

Even today, the government and central banks have an intense interest in not allowing the gold price to send a no-confidence signal to the world of just how weak the dollar is. Central banks in recent years have been selling constantly, and I'm strongly suspicious that the President's Working Group on Financial Markets—the "Plunge Protection Team"—participates in the gold market as well to keep the price suppressed.

As recently as November 2008, Bernanke admitted to me in a Financial Services Committee hearing that the only time gold is discussed with other central bankers is for the purpose of selling—never to consider its merit in serving as a reserve for a new currency agreement.

Before gold became legal to own in 1975, many gold bugs were buying it. I purchased my first gold shortly after the breakdown of the Bretton Woods Agreement. The law was circumvented by buying numismatic coins (any coin dated 1947 or older was considered a numismatic coin). Mexico accommodated American citizens by minting the beautiful Mexican 50 peso, weighing 1.2 ounces, and placing the date 1947 on it. The coins I bought at that time for financial security I still have, and now they are getting close to being legitimate numismatic coins.

Jim Blanchard almost single-handedly led the successful effort to legalize gold ownership. He held his first gold conference in 1974 in New Orleans and I attended this conference. A small crowd of a few hundred was expected, but a much larger crowd of more than 700 showed up.

It was there I met Hans Sennholz, one of the speakers. Sennholz was one of only six individuals who received a PhD under Mises. I got to know Sennholz over the years, attending events in Grove City where he was the chairman of the Economics Department. He even came for a campaign event for me in 1974, which I recall was totally perplexing to my campaign manager, who was not exactly into gold and the Federal Reserve. When Sennholz was president of the Foundation for Economic Education (FEE) after retiring from Grove City College, he had me join the board, which prompted a few visits to FEE's headquarters in Irvington-on-Hudson, New York.

In 1974, I had met and came to respect highly Leonard Read, founder of FEE. He served a great purpose following World War II in keeping the freedom movement alive and encouraging many others to participate in this crucial endeavor. Leonard was much more interested in education than politics. Even so, once I was in Congress, he had me visit FEE on a couple of occasions. I'm sure he was pleased I was in Congress, but he understood, as I do, that education is the key to political change. I have no problem with those who say education is the most important thing, but eventually a theoretical philosophy has to be translated into political actions—and that's exactly what the Founders did.

Mises had something to say about this: "The flowering of human society depends on two factors; the intellectual power of outstanding men to conceive sound, social and economic theories and the ability of these or other men to make these ideologies palatable to the majority."[4]

In my opinion, the political leaders must make the ideology acceptable to the people. Of course, the ideology of welfare and socialism is easier to sell since it's based on the majority getting something for free. But when the people recognize that's only a temporary situation they will become more open to the suggestion that freedom offers more, once the bankruptcy of statism is acknowledged. Such a condition is becoming more apparent every day.

4. Ludwig von Mises, *Human Action* (New Haven, CT: Yale University Press, 1949), p. 863.

Making an ideology palatable to the majority means the people must come to realize that their best interests are served by its acceptance. In the case of freedom, the consensus of the people must be that self-reliance, free markets, private property, sound money, and enforceable contracts are indispensable to prosperity, peace, and happiness.

Central economic planning and false promises must be rejected. Some, on principle, will always reject the temptation to use government power to enhance their own position; others will reject it when it's clear that the prosperity promised, based on lies, fraud, and force, can only be temporarily provided. Transfer of wealth through government force is self-limited. The appearance of wealth by borrowing and inflation always leads to heartache and suffering. An opportunity has arrived for our "sound social and economic theories" to be made available and acceptable to the majority.

Of all the Austrian economic greats of the twentieth century, I got to know Murray Rothbard the best. During my first tour of duty in Congress (1976–1984), while Lew Rockwell, founder of the Mises Institute, was serving as my chief of staff, we contacted Murray and invited him to Washington in 1979 for a visit. On his first trip, as he watched our office in action, I recall him saying he was amazed that a member of Congress actually made a determined effort to understand the details of each piece of legislation in the context of the Constitution. I recall his surprise when he found out I had read his essay "Gold and Fluctuating Fiat Exchange Rates." From this early association, he and Lew Rockwell went on to participate in many projects, the most important one being the establishment of the Mises Institute.

Murray was a good teacher, and I have frequently said that his book *America's Great Depression* was a real eye-opener for me, as was his classic *What Has Government Done to Our Money?*[5] Having been raised in a Republican home, I was taught to believe Hoover's failure was a result of noncooperation by the Democrats in Congress. Murray thoroughly rebutted that notion with his explanation of how Hoover and FDR endorsed the same flawed policies of economic intervention and both were responsible for prolonging the Depression, which was precipitated by the seriously flawed monetary policy of the Federal Reserve in the 1920s.

If there's one book that the Washington establishment should read now, it's Rothbard's book *America's Great Depression*.[6] In this book, he demonstrates that it was the Fed that created the late-1920s boom that led to bust, and Hoover's interventions that prolonged the Great Depression. (Murray, interestingly, was on my congressional staff during the time that the Gold Commission was meeting in 1981.)

Murray, along with businessman Burt Blumert and Lew Rockwell, influenced my decision to run as the Libertarian candidate for President in 1988. That project, like all political projects, was filled with frustrations and shortcomings. Nevertheless, we all considered it a worthwhile effort in building the case for liberty. Obviously, the reception for the message in 1988 was subdued compared to the enthusiastic reception we got in the 2008 race. Conditions have greatly changed. But the

5. Murray N. Rothbard, *What Has Government Done to Our Money?* (Auburn, AL: Mises Institute, 2005, 1963).

6. Murray N. Rothbard, *America's Great Depression* (Auburn, AL: Mises Institute, 2009, 1963).

Republican versus the Libertarian approach was also a factor, given monopoly control of the electoral process. Today, the field is much more fertile for our ideas. Many seeds have been planted over these past two decades, and the effort is now bearing fruit.

Shortly before Murray died on January 7, 1995, I called him to tell him of my plans to run for Congress once again in the 1996 election. He was extremely excited and very encouraging. Unlike Leonard Read, Murray loved politics, Republican or Libertarian, or whatever he found of interest at any particular time. He got into the minutia of internecine activities that were beyond my interest. He always knew all the players and their perceived intentions and philosophical motivations. He played politics in the 1992 Republican primary in support of Pat Buchanan in a coalition of sorts, when Pat opposed the first war on Iraq and George H. W. Bush's tax increases.

One thing I am certain of—if Murray could have been with us during the presidential primary in 2008, he would have had a lot to say about it and fun saying it. He would have been very excited. His natural tendency to be optimistic would have been enhanced. He would have loved every minute of it. He would have pushed the "revolution," especially since he contributed so much to preparing for it.

I can just imagine how enthralled he would have been to see college kids burning Federal Reserve notes. He would have led the chant we heard at so many rallies: "End the Fed! End the Fed!"

Even after the presidential campaign, the momentum has generated an interest in a serious movement to expose the Fed for the purposes of ending it, and Murray would be pleased. His intellectual effort would have been vindicated. Ideas were being translated into a serious effort to bring about a major political and economic change. His books, and especially his smaller booklets designed for broader distribution, on why the Fed must be ended and a 100 percent gold standard be required, have served us well. And they will continue to do so. His books *What Has Government Done to Our Money? The Case for a 100 Percent Gold Dollar*, and *The Case Against the Fed*[7] have been invaluable assets in educating the general public.

Murray told a lot of stories about his time in the Ayn Rand "cult" and his association with Greenspan. Greenspan did acknowledge to me in private conversation his acquaintance with Murray. But think of the different outcomes. Both started as followers of Ayn Rand. Neither became an objectivist. Greenspan went the wrong way. Rothbard went the right way, always perfecting the truth regarding money and the Federal Reserve.

Greenspan became a monetary tyrant who sowed the seeds of the greatest financial bubble in all of history.

During this period of searching for the answers about money and Austrian economics, I also met Henry Hazlitt, who was a friend of Mises's, a board member of FEE, and a close associate of Leonard Read's. Like so many others looking for answers, I read his famous *Economics in One Lesson*. Mr. Hazlitt, shortly after the 1944 Bretton Woods Agreement was signed, predicted it would not work, and he lived well past the time to see its breakdown in 1971. Like many Austrian economists, he lived to an old age (ninety-eight); he

---

7. Murray N. Rothbard, *The Case Against the Fed* (Auburn, AL: Mises Institute, 1994).

died in 1993. All his books, of which there are many, are worth reading.

Hazlitt was instrumental in securing a position at New York University for Mises. He had befriended Mises on his arrival to the United States after Mises escaped from Europe as World War II erupted. Although he was for years known as a journalist for *Newsweek*, the *New York Times*, and the *Wall Street Journal*, Hazlitt was in reality a philosopher and economist.

His greatest compliment to me was after Leonard Read's death in 1983; he called and asked if I might consider becoming president of FEE. Whether anyone else on the FEE board shared this thought, I don't know, but it was something I never seriously considered, simply because I had chosen a different educational path.

Another interesting tidbit of history was that Henry Hazlitt introduced Ayn Rand to all the free-market scholars in New York, which included his close friends Leonard Read and Mises.

The period between the Depression and the end of Bretton Woods in 1971 was a time of much activity by many very smart, libertarian, and old right constitutionalists and noninterventionists. They lamented the destruction of the Republic, but their writings laid the foundation of the emerging freedom movement that became so energized during the Republican primary elections of 2008.

And there were many others I read that kept the spirit of the Republic alive. Some were much more interested in monetary policy, while others talked about personal liberty and foreign policy as well as economic liberty. Having read the books of John T. Flynn, Isabel Patterson, Rose Wilder Lane, Garet Garrett, Ayn Rand, Richard Weaver, Albert J. Nock, H. L.

Mencken, and Frank Chodorov, I was not only influenced but convinced that a philosophy that embraced personal liberty, private property, and sound money was the only political philosophy worth championing.

To understand the need for sound money and no central bank, one must fully understand the principles of liberty. There were also several members of Congress during this period who held their ground and voted in keeping with the Constitution: Dr. Smith of Ohio, Howard Buffett, and H. R. Gross.

We all owe a great deal of gratitude to the men and women who did such a superb job of presenting the moral case for liberty and refuting all the monstrous lies, ignorance, and arrogance of those who spent their lives promoting authoritarianism, statism, and universal use of aggressive force.

Although Ayn Rand never spoke kindly of libertarians and I never contemplated becoming a supporter of objectivism as a total philosophy, I did read all her novels and received her objectivist newsletter essentially the whole time it was published. She challenged many of my beliefs that I had taken for granted and forced me to understand and defend them better. However, she never convinced me of her definition and application of altruism. Equating voluntary Christian charities with Communism made no sense to me. But she also built up my excitement for championing freedom. I have in my library a copy of the original 1957 hardbound edition of her huge *Atlas Shrugged*. The price listed on the cover flap is $6.95. There's no doubt she influenced a lot of people over the decades and forced them to reassess their premises, and most came away being more devoted to liberty.

CHAPTER 4

CENTRAL BANKS AND WAR

Following the creation of the Fed, the government would discover other uses for an elastic money supply aside from keeping the banking system from defaulting on its obligations. It would prove useful in funding war. It is no coincidence that the century of total war coincided with the century of central banking. When governments had to fund their own wars without a paper money machine to rely upon, they economized on resources. They found diplomatic solutions to prevent war, and after they started a war they ended it as soon as possible.

But for European governments in the late nineteenth century, the fiscal limits on war were removed. Now with central banks, governments could just print what they needed, and therefore they were more willing to pull the trigger and pick fights. The diplomats were powerless to stop governments itching to try out their newfound funding machines. Might a diplomatic solution have been found for the struggles that led to World War I had the Germans and English not had recourse to the printing press and a lender of last resort?

Counterfactual history is always difficult but it is an interesting question to ask.

As Mises wrote in 1919, "one can say without exaggeration that inflation is an indispensable means of militarism. Without it, the repercussions of war on welfare become obvious much more quickly and penetratingly; war weariness would set in much earlier."[1]

Armed with central banks to cover liabilities, European governments began a war one year after the Fed was created. The *New York Tribune* wrote with horror: "The world looks on in a stunned, incredulous way while Europe is rushing forward to a stupendous catastrophe. . . . We have been told again and again that the financiers of the world, largely denationalized in their sympathies and interests, would never permit the great nations to impoverish themselves by a general war. A tightening of the screws of credit, it has been said, would bring most chancelleries to their senses."[2]

It was once so, but central banking changed that forever. No more would governments be bound by the fear of bankruptcy and financial ruin. The magic of inflationary finance would provide for them no matter what.

So, too, in an earlier time, the United States might have stayed out of the European conflict. But having the Fed, the United States entered the war in 1917, and with it came the most centralized experiment in national economic planning

1. Ludwig von Mises, *Nation, State, and Economy* (New York: New York University Press, 1983), p. 163.

2. Cited in Groseclose, *America's Money Machine: The Story of the Federal Reserve* (Westport, CT: Arlington House, 1966), p. 88.

to date. There were price controls, new taxes, government nationalization of railroads, the War Industries Board, Liberty Loans, new bonds to float, and a massive expansion of government debt that was backed by the power of the Fed to create money to pay back the debt.

In those days, the Fed did not have the power to create money through the discount window, but it did serve that important role of being a guarantor of the government's debts. It was the lender of last resort, and it had plenty of capacity for creating new money out of thin air. The monetary expansion began in December 1914 and America went through the first of many false booms. Interest rates were pegged low at the very time when they should have been rising due to greater risk.

As Friedman and Schwartz report concerning World War I:[3]

> The stock of money, which had been rising at a moderate rate throughout 1914, started to rise at an increasing rate in early 1915, rose most rapidly, as prices did, from late 1915 to mid-1917, and then resumed its rapid rise before the end of 1918, rather sooner than prices did. At its peak in June 1920, the stock of money was roughly double its September 1915 level and more than double the level of November 1914, when the Federal Reserve Banks opened for business.

3. Milton Friedman and Anna J. Schwartz, *A Monetary History of the United States, 1857–1960* (Princeton, NJ: Princeton University Press, 1963), p. 198.

Banks began to offer public credit to buy government bonds. The price level also expanded dramatically in response to monetary inflation. The false boom continued through 1918 until the war came to an end. The nation immediately went into recession, followed by another miniature boom-bust cycle from 1920 to 1921. In total, scholars have estimated that only 21 percent of the war was funded through taxation. The remainder was funded by Fed-backed borrowing (56 percent) and outright money creation (23 percent), for a total cost of $33 billion.

So we see that the damage that the Fed wrought came rather quickly after its creation. Compared with today, its power was limited then. But the goal of creating a lender of last resort had a devastating effect on our public policy. It inspired the government to dream of ever more power, ever more programs, ever more ambitions. So long as the funding was there, there would be no restraining the state, even when people with fiscally conservative impulses entered into leadership roles.

Never forget what the "Great War" meant for Europe. It meant the end of the old monarchies, a relatively peaceful world that was centralized in name only and decentralized in practice, and the beginning of warlike democratic states organized along technocratic lines. For the United States, it meant the entrenchment of the imperial presidency and a globalized foreign policy mission. For Germany, it created the conditions of the great inflation, which led to Hitler coming to power based on the fomenting of national resentment.

For Russia, it meant the beginning of Communism.

Lew Rockwell explains how:[4]

The Russian war itself was funded through money cre-ation, which also led to massive price increases and controls and shortages during the war . . . the temptation that the money machine provided the regime proved too inviting. It turned a relatively benign monarchy into a war machine. A country that had long been integrated into the worldwide division of labor and was under a gold standard became a killing machine. And as horrific and catastrophic as the war dead were for Russian morale, the inflation affected every last person and inspired massive unrest that led to the triumph of Communism.

In the United States, it fundamentally altered the balance of power in our democratic system. Votes, campaign promises, polls, public opinion, laws, restrictions on the state, all of these forces took a backseat to the goals of the government to expand. Imagine an irresponsible teenager with an unlimited line of credit. The parents, teachers, pastors, and authorities in his life are ultimately powerless to change his habits. Now imagine that teenager armed to the teeth and also immune even from the rule of law. This is what we have with a government backed by a central bank.

A good example of this occurred at the end of World War I. The public was sickened by the loss of freedom that they had

4. Llewellyn H. Rockwell, Jr., "War and Inflation," speech delivered at the Future of Freedom Foundation's conference Restoring the Republic, Reston, Virginia, June 6, 2008, posted at http://mises.org/story/3010.

seen, and people demanded more accountability from government and more freedom in civic and economic affairs. Government spending fell dramatically, and there were hearings in Congress to ferret out those who had profited from war. The mood was captured by Warren Harding's 1920 campaign slogan, "A return to normalcy." An example of a bestselling book that reflected the postwar and interwar mood is *Merchants of Death: A Study of the International Armament Industry.*[5]

Sadly, however, there would never be normalcy again so long as a central bank stood ready to fund a government of abnormal powers. The old rules no longer applied. The beast that promised all things to all people, made the wishes of all politicians come true, made life easy for the money creators, and promised funding for every unconstrained vision was already created. Whatever anyone demanded from the government could be granted. What's more, the banking establishment in this country enjoyed new guarantees against failure, which created a "moral hazard" for them. Their lending activities would proceed without due consideration of risk.

To understand the Roaring Twenties, then, it is also important to look at the role of the Fed in monetary policy. The average annual increase in the money stock ranged between 7.3 percent and 8.1 percent, for a total increase of between 55 and 61 percent.[6] It was inevitable that this false boom would lead to a bust, first in the most fashionable sector of the economy—the stock market—and spreading through the entire sector.

President Hoover in 1930 might have done what was done

5. H. C. Engelbrecht and F. C. Hanighen, *Merchants of Death* (New York: Dodd, Mead & Co., 1934).

6. For details on calculating money aggregates in the 1920s, see Murray N. Rothbard, *America's Great Depression* (Auburn, AL: Mises Institute, 2009, 1963).

in 1920: essentially the government didn't try to bail out the system. The Fed wasn't yet in full swing and was actually somewhat reluctant to inflate without limit. Contrary to myth, however, Hoover actually undertook a huge effort to bail out the system using the monetary tools of the time. That they were not effective in doing so was beside the point: he tried to inflate the United States out of recession (in addition to raising taxes, imposing new trade restrictions, and more such interventions).

Franklin Roosevelt merely followed up on the Hoover antirecession plan, and went even further in destroying the nation's money system. He closed the banks, made private gold ownership illegal, and dealt a massive blow to what was left of the gold standard. The New Deal did not end the Depression. Unemployment was as high before World War II as it was in 1932, and incomes and productivity had actually declined. But the Fed was more powerful than ever, standing ready to fund yet another war.

Since World War II, the U.S. government has expanded its reach with a shocking voraciousness both at home and abroad. It's been one war after another, the building of killer weapons of mass destruction, the construction of a huge welfare state that covers all classes in society. There was the Cold War, the Korean War, the Bay of Pigs, an invasion of the Dominican Republic, Vietnam, and endless involvement in the Middle East in addition to wars on Nicaragua, Salvador, Bosnia, and Haiti, as well as all the wars around the world conducted in the name of the War on Terror. And after every major crisis, whether 9/11, the dot-com disaster of 1999, or the economic meltdown of 2008, the response is more monetary expansion.

It was once thought that the government had to choose between providing guns or butter. Now, with the Fed, it is realized that no such choice is ultimately necessary. Politicians get together and agree to logroll so that each special interest is able to get what it wants. Guns, butter, and everything else under the sun, including endless bailouts of failing businesses as well as foreign aid for the world, are all provided courtesy of the money machine. Even when the Fed is not providing direct infusions of newly created money, it stands ready to back endless creations of debt year after year, none of which would be worth anything on the free-market bond market if the Fed were not there to guarantee it all.

The Fed is what has made this crisis-response model possible, for without the money machine standing by to provide all the funding that the powerful people need, none of this would be possible. The American people would have to be taxed, and I doubt that they would stand for too many tax increases along these lines. Disguise this tax increase in the form of monetary expansion and you can provide government funding and spread the costs throughout society.

The Fed is not alone among the failed central banks of the world. The interwar period also created catastrophic hyperinflations in Germany, Austria, Russia, Poland, and Hungary.[7] The promises of the glorious world created by central banking were in tatters. But by then, governments were hooked on the loose-credit drug and would not restore sound money.

The longer we delay a conversion to sound money and away from central banking, the worse our crises will grow and the more government will expand at the expense of our liberties.

7. David Hackett Fischer, *The Great Wave: Price Revolutions and the Rhythm of History* (New York: Oxford University Press, 1996), p. 193.

CHAPTER 5

THE GOLD COMMISSION

There is no denying that the subject of gold is central to the issue of restoring sound money. That's because gold emerged from within the structure of the market economy as the most important guarantor of the quality of money. It was not chosen by governments but by the market. The reason is easy to understand. Gold has all the qualities that we associate most with good money: divisibility, portability, high value per unit of weight, durability, and uniform quality.

Whenever I talk of a gold standard, there are always people ready to accuse me of having some obsession or fixation. *Fetish* is a word thrown around. In fact, I'm only observing reality: the idea of sound money in most of human history has been bound up with gold money. Can there be sound money without a gold standard? In principle, yes. And I'd be very happy for a system that would permit markets to once again choose the most suitable money, whatever that turns out to be. I'm not for government imposing any particular standard: no central bank, no legal tender, no privilege for any commodity chosen as a backing for the currency.

And yet the reality is that the dollar is money, even if the quality of the dollar is very poor. I've always believed that government has a responsibility to restore what it has destroyed. In the late 1970s, many people began to agree. I coauthored with Jesse Helms the legislation that passed in the closing days of the Carter administration to form the Gold Commission. The commission was not organized until after President Reagan took office. Of its seventeen members, Lewis Lehrman and Arthur Costamagna were the only others who were sympathetic to gold. The rest were antigold politicians, Fed members, and Treasury officials.

Secretary of the Treasury Donald Regan was the chairman of the committee and presided over our first meeting on July 16, 1981. Interestingly enough, that first meeting was off the record, without the media, and no minutes were taken. The plan to keep all meetings secret and without minutes was revealed to the public with the help of columnist Bob Novak and others, and there was a bit of a public uproar. Due to public pressure, a vote of the committee membership showed overwhelming support for open hearings.

Henry Reuss, chairman of the House Banking Committee, attended one meeting and left in a rage. He couldn't stand one minute of serious consideration of the importance of gold. Before ownership of gold was made legal once again in the United States, which occurred in 1975, Reuss predicted that if it were to occur, gold would drop to $5 an ounce and the "gold bugs" should be happy with the government propping the price up at $35 an ounce. He, of course, had it wrong; it was the artificially low price of gold that was propping up the value of the dollar—at least temporarily.

By the time of our first hearing, gold had topped $800 an ounce. Reuss was not in a good frame of mind. He had been given a pro-gold newsletter by an attendee that prompted his outburst. As he left, he crumpled up the newsletter, tossed it, and let out a tirade attacking the commission's purpose. Let it be recorded that though there was little sympathy on the committee for gold, Reuss won the award for being the most hostile to the thought that gold could replace the "wisdom" of the Federal Reserve Board and "wise" chairmen of the Banking Committee.

At the time, no one seriously believed we were on the verge of restoring some relationship of the dollar to gold, yet there was deep concern regarding the dollar, inflation, and the very weak economy. The worries were great, but compared to the fear felt today, there's no comparison, and for good reason.

In 1981 we had only been operating with the fiat dollar reserve standard for ten years. Today, we've had the imbalances build up for thirty-eight years. In some ways the painful adjustments of the 1970s were helpful for the short term. The need for dollar devaluation was recognized. Fluctuating exchange rates, as disruptive as they were, provided a "market" mechanism that was better tolerated than the pretense of artificially fixed exchange rates. In other words, a token market mechanism was helpful to prop up a very fragile system.

I recall vividly an event following one particular meeting of the Gold Commission at the Treasury Building. The Houston Republican delegation made plans to attend a Republican function in Houston, along with President Reagan. We were to meet Reagan at Andrews Air Force Base and fly on Air Force One to Houston. Due to the commission's hearing at the Treasury Building, which is across the street from the White House, my staff arranged for me to walk across the street and fly with President Reagan on Marine One to Andrews. That way I wouldn't miss any part of the hearings and could still travel to Houston for the Republican meeting.

On the helicopter flight to Andrews, the subject of the gold standard naturally came up. "Ron," the President told me, "no great nation that abandoned the gold standard has remained a great nation." He indeed was sympathetic, as he was to many libertarian constitutional ideas, but he was also swayed by staff pressure to be pragmatic on most issues.

Arthur Costamagna, a friend of Reagan's and a member of the commission signed on our dissenting views with a minor qualification. Lew Lehrman, later to run for governor of New York, signed as well. Then my staff and I scheduled a meeting with the President, the goal of which was to present him a copy and get a photo opportunity. The meeting was scheduled without a specific purpose, and I didn't want to surprise him with my plan. We called back to clarify the intent of the meeting. It wasn't too long after that that we received a callback from the White House staff saying that the meeting was canceled. The presentation and picture taking never occurred.

I'm sure Jim Baker, and especially Don Regan, made sure that it did not take place. Don Regan, as chairman of the Gold Commission, was the one who demanded the whole series of hearings be kept secret without minutes. The first report was filed March 31, 1982.

The political system essentially works this way. Staff, if not perfectly loyal to the philosophy of the officeholder, can block progress. Ultimately, though, the responsibility falls on the officeholder to pick the right staff.

Surviving the 1970s gave the dollar a reprieve and set the stage for one giant financial bubble to be formed over the next twenty-seven years to get us to today. If, as a result of the Gold Commission, we had returned to our senses in 1981, the problems and grave dangers we now face could have been averted.

Murray Rothbard argued in his testimony before the commission that it was not the gold standard that caused the Depression of the 1930s; rather, it was the misuse of the gold standard that led up to it. In the closing part of his statement, he urged that if gold were ever to return as a standard, it must be a gold coin standard where citizens have the right to have their paper currency redeemed in gold coins.

Alan Greenspan also testified, and it was a rather decent statement; although he did not call for a gold standard, he advocated issuing treasury bonds that were backed by gold as an interim step in moving in that direction. In 1981, he was not as strong for the gold standard as he was in the 1960s, but not as hostile as he became later on.

Hans Sennholz also submitted a statement to the Gold Commission. He, of course, was a strong supporter of the gold standard, but he was perceptive in not being very optimistic about it occurring in the near future. Sennholz said: "They are indulging in daydreaming when they envision an early return (to the gold standard). The fiat money forces are much too strong and public support for deficit spending yet too powerful to expect the currency reform in the foreseeable future."

Of course, if support for deficit spending was strong in 1981, all we need do is take a look at the pressures today to spend money that we don't have. It will be a while before there's serious consideration for currency reform associated with a restructuring of the worldwide financial system. But the day is fast approaching when it won't be out of choice but out of necessity that we will have to face this issue.

There will be no new Gold Commission, no open discussion regarding gold as money in the current administration. There will be, behind the scenes, the Fed and other elites planning a new system, international in scope and fiat in nature. It will not be smooth sailing, considering the task at hand.

The countries with the greatest financial and military might will have the most influence, as the United States has had since World War II. Our military might remains supreme. Our economic strength is still first, but the trends tell us that that won't last. Without economic strength and currency superiority, the military might well be steadily diminished. Although we'll not see a second Gold Commission, one more serious than the first, the intellectual fight between fiat money and commodity money will rage, and the winner will decide our economic fate and what kind of society we will be living in.

Paul Volcker was called to stop inflation and restore confidence in the dollar in the 1970s, which to a large degree he did. It was in 1982, when the Fed turned on the monetary spigots once again, that we returned to the boom-bust cycles. In some ways, the sophistication of the Fed in controlling necessary corrections created a false sense of security. Many came to believe Greenspan to be a great maestro of the economy; his reputation soared among Republicans and Democrats.

Many, including Greenspan, believed that a new economic

paradigm was upon us. There was a belief that serious economic downturns could be prevented by wise monetary policy. But their "wise monetary policy" had nothing to do with sound money or interest rates and credit being determined by the market. The economic planners literally believed that there would never be a price to pay for inflating a currency, manipulating interest rates, and monetizing debt. In reality, this "sophistication" in managing the economy was merely postponing the inevitable consequences, and it guaranteed they would be much worse.

One of the wonderful products of the Gold Commission was our minority report, which remains in print today.[1] Only three members of the Gold Commission signed it, but the full committee recommended to Congress to mint a gold coin. Since gold was legal to own by Americans once again, this was a concession to the pro-gold supporters around the country. In addition, it was meant to challenge the near monopoly of the South African Krugerrand being sold in the United States.

I argued for a gold coin without a dollar denomination stated as legal tender. I wanted people to think of money as a weight. My ultimate goal is to repeal legal tender laws. It's just as well, though, that I lost that argument, since some are now testing the legal tender status of this coin by forcing it into circulation at face value.

By the time the coin bill was finally passed in 1985, as a result of our effort in the Gold Commission, I was no longer

---

1. Ron Paul and Lewis Lehrman, *The Case for Gold* (Auburn, AL: Mises Institute, 2007, 1983).

in Congress. I introduced the original bill, but I left Congress at the end of 1984. Later there was a separate bill to mint the Silver Eagle.

The bill authorized the minting of gold coins in four sizes: 1 ounce, $1/2$ ounce, $1/4$ ounce, and $1/10$ ounce. The 1 ounce coin was legal tender for $50, the $1/2$ ounce was $25, the $1/4$ ounce was $10, and the $1/10$ ounce was $5. Do a little bit of arithmetic and you realize the $1/4$ ounce or $10 coin makes no sense at all. Those who made the final decision on the bill wanted it to be confusing. The one ounce of silver made legal tender for $1 further compounds the problem of defining a dollar when compared to a Federal Reserve note, an old silver dollar, or a Double Eagle.

Making the coins legal tender was ridiculous and nonsensical and was done to guarantee that people wouldn't consider paying a $50 debt with an ounce of gold, nor would they do it with silver dollars.

I always assumed that the IRS would never accept for tax purposes true exchange at the face value of the new coins. But some enterprising and brave constitutionalists challenged this law in Las Vegas and paid the employees in silver and gold coins, and taxes were reported at the much lower level. Many paid no tax due to the lower minimum wage. As expected, it was challenged in court, and miraculously, litigants "won" their case in a hung jury. The silliness of our legal tender laws and the impossibility of defining a "dollar" convinced the jury that those charged did not commit fraud and it was the confusion of the law that was at fault.

We have not yet heard the final word in this challenge. I'm delighted it's being fought, and any favorable precedent may be helpful if an economic breakdown occurs and a lot more people do the same thing. But courts, as they did in the Civil War and the 1930s, have always ruled in favor of the tyrants when push comes to shove in dealing with the money issue. My bet is the government will not permit the use of new gold and silver bullion coins, that is, until the End the Fed revolution comes to fruition.

CHAPTER 6

CONVERSATIONS WITH GREENSPAN

Over the years I've had many interesting interchanges with Federal Reserve chairmen. The most occurred with Alan Greenspan. He fascinated me the most because of my early exposure to his support for the gold standard and disdain for the Federal Reserve and paper money.

I was a subscriber to Ayn Rand's objectivist newspaper of the 1960s and studied closely Greenspan's 1966 article "Gold and Economic Freedom" in that publication.[1] I told him that he had made a favorable impression on me—once. He always was aware of exactly where I was coming from, and at times, even when I did not explicitly mention gold in my questions, he would answer in the context of the gold standard. Although frequently annoyed, and more so as the years went on, he never seemed quite as annoyed or dismayed as Ben Bernanke is with my questions.

Greenspan's claim, in an answer to one of my questions, was that the central bankers essentially had become smart

1. Ayn Rand, *Capitalism: The Unknown Ideal* (New York, New American Library, 1967).

enough to achieve all the benefits of the gold standard without its limitations. Of course, it's the limitations that are so valuable, and the reason the gold standard is so important to a free society. These thoughts he stated brilliantly in his own historic article, "Gold and Economic Freedom":

> In the absence of the gold standard, there is no way to protect savings from confiscation through inflation. There is no safe store of value. If there were, the government would have to make its holding illegal, as was done in the case of gold. If everyone decided, for example, to convert all his bank deposits as silver or copper or any other good and thereafter decline to accept checks as payments for goods, bank deposits would lose their purchasing power and government-credited bank credit would be worthless as claims on goods. The financial policy of the welfare state requires that there be no way for the owners of wealth to protect themselves.
>
> This is the shabby secret of the welfare statists' tirades against gold. Deficit spending is simply a scheme for the confiscation of wealth. Gold stands in the way of this insidious process. It stands as a protector of property rights. If one grasps this, one has no difficulty in understanding the statists' antagonism toward the gold standard.

According to his own logic, Greenspan had simply become a statist.

I once asked Greenspan about his views on the work of Mises and the Austrian economists. Here is a transcript from June 25, 2000.

RON PAUL: Basically, the way I understand the Austrian free market explanation of a business cycle is once we embark on inflation, the creation of new money, we distort interest rates and we cause people to do dumb things. They overinvest, there is malinvestment, there is overcapacity and there has to be a correction, and the many good members or well-known members of the Austrian school, I am sure you are well aware of them, Mises, Hayek, and Rothbard, as well as Henry Hazlitt, have written about this, and really did a pretty good job on predicting. It was the reason I was attracted to their writing, because certainly, Mises understood clearly that the Soviet system wouldn't work.

In the 1920s, the Austrian economic policy explained what would probably come in the 1930s. None of the Austrian economists were surprised about the bursting of the bubble in Japan in 1989, and Japan, by the way, had surpluses. And, of course, the best prediction of the Austrian economists was the breakdown of the Bretton Woods Agreement, and that certainly told us something about what to expect in the 1970s.

But the concerns from that school of thought would be that we still are inflating. Between 1995 and 1999, our M3 money supply went up 41 percent. It increased during that period of time twice as fast as the GDP, contributing to this condition that we have. We have had benefits as a reserve currency of the world, which allows us to perpetuate the bubble, the financial bubble. Because of our huge current account deficit, we are now borrowing more than a billion dollars a day to finance, you know, our prosperity, and most economists, whether they are from the Austrian school or not, would accept the notion that this is unsustainable and something would have to happen.

Even recently I saw a statistic that showed total bank credit out of the realm of day-to-day activity in control of the Fed is increasing at the rate of 22 percent. We are now the biggest debtor in the world. We have $1.5 trillion foreign debt, and that now is 20 percent of the GDP, and these statistics concern many of the economists as a foreboding of things to come.

And my question dealing with this is, where do the Austrian economists go wrong? And where do you criticize them and say that we can't accept anything that they say?

My second question deals with productivity. There are various groups that have said that our statistics are off. Estevao and Lach claim, and this was written up in the St. Louis Fed pamphlet, that the temps aren't considered and that distorts the views. Stephen Roach at Morgan Stanley said we don't take into consideration overtime. Robert Gordon of Northwestern University says that 99 percent of the productivity benefits were in the computer industry and had very little to do with the general economy, and therefore, we should not be anxious to reassure ourselves that the productive increases will protect us from future corrections that could be rather serious.

ALAN GREENSPAN: Well, I will be glad to give you a long academic discussion on the Austrian school and its implications with respect to modern views of how the economy works having actually attended a seminar of Ludwig Mises, when he was probably ninety, and I was a very small fraction of that. So I was aware of a great deal of what those teachings were, and a lot of them still are right. There is no question that they have been absorbed into the general view of the academic profession in many different ways, and you can see a goodly part of the teachings of the Austrian school in many of the academic materials that come out in today's various journals, even though they are rarely, if ever, discussed in those terms.

We have an extraordinary economy with which we have to deal both in the United States and the rest of the world. What we find over the generations is that the underlying forces which engender economic change themselves are changing all the time, human nature being the sole apparent constant throughout the whole process. I think it is safe to say that economists generally continuously struggle to understand which particular structure is essentially defining what makes the economy likely to move in one direction or another in the period immediately ahead, and I will venture to say that that view continuously changes from one decade to the next. We had views about inflation in the 1960s, and in fact, the desirability of a little inflation, which we no longer hold anymore, at least the vast majority no longer hold as being desirable.

The general elements which contribute to stability in a market economy change from period to period as we observe that certain hypotheses about how the system works do not square with reality. So all I can say is that the long tentacles, you might say, of the Austrian school have reached far into the future from when most of them practiced and have had a profound and, in my judgment, probably an irreversible effect on how most mainstream economists think in this country.

RON PAUL: You don't have time to answer the one on productivity, but in some ways, I am sort of hoping you would say don't worry about these Austrian economists, because if you worry too much about them, and these predictions they paint in the past came true, in some ways we should be concerned, and I would like you to reassure me that they are absolutely wrong.

ALAN GREENSPAN: Let me distinguish between analyses of the way economies work and forecasts people make as a consequence of those analyses. The remarkable thing about the behavior of economies is they rarely square with forecasts as much as one should hope they did. I know there is a big dispute on the issue of productivity data. I don't want to get into that. We would be here for the rest of the month. I think the evidence, in my judgment, is increasingly persuasive that there has been an indeed underlying structural change in productivity in this country.

Prior to one of our biannual meetings with Greenspan, we were given a photo opportunity. Since it was a scheduled event, I brought with me my copy of the original faded green objectivist newspaper of 1966. During the short visit and picture taking, I showed him a copy of the letter and asked if he recalled the newsletter, which he quickly acknowledged.

Upon opening the small booklet to his "Gold and Economic Freedom" article, I asked if he would autograph the article for me, which he promptly did. As he was signing the article, I asked if he would like to put a disclaimer on it. Astoundingly, he answered that he had just recently reread it and wouldn't change a word of it.

In a hearing July 21, 2004, the exchange in which I discussed the housing bubble went as follows:

RON PAUL: As the economy slowed in 2000, 2001, of course, there was an aggressive approach by inflating and lowering the interest rates to an unprecedented level of 1 percent. But lo and behold, when we look back at this, we find out that manufacturing really hasn't recovered, savings hasn't recovered, the housing bubble continues, the current account deficit is way out of whack, continuing to grow as our foreign debt grew, and consumer debt is rising as well as government debt.

So it looks like this 1 percent really hasn't done much good other than prevent the deflating of the bubble, which means that, yes, we have had a temporary victory, but we have delayed the inevitable, the pain and suffering that must always come after the distortion occurs from a period of time of inflating.

So my question to you is: how unique do you think this period of time is that we live in and the job that you have? To me, it is not surprising that half the people think you are too early and the other half think you are too late on raising rates. But since fiat money has never survived for long periods of time in all of history, is it possible that the funnel of tasks that you face today is a historic event, possibly the beginning of the end of the fiat system that replaced Bretton Woods thirty-three years ago? And since there is no evidence that fiat money works in the long run, is there any possibility that you would entertain that, quote, "We may have to address the subject of overall monetary policy not only domestically but internationally in order to restore real growth"?

ALAN GREENSPAN: Well, Congressman, you are raising the more fundamental question as to being on a commodity standard or another standard. And this issue has been debated, as you know as well as I, extensively for a significant period of time.

Once you decide that a commodity standard such as the gold standard is, for whatever reasons, not acceptable in a society and you go to a fiat currency, then the question is automatically, unless you have government endeavoring to determine the supply of the currency, it is very difficult to create what effectively the gold standard did.

I think you will find, as I have indicated to you before, that most effective central banks in this fiat money period tend to be successful largely because we tend to replicate that which would probably have occurred under a commodity standard in general.

I have stated in the past that I have always thought that fiat currencies by their nature are inflationary. I was taken aback by observing the fact that, from the early 1990s forward, Japan demonstrated that fact not to be a broad universal principle. And what I have begun to realize is that, because we tend to replicate a good deal of what a commodity standard would do, we are not getting the long-term inflationary consequences of fiat money. I will tell you, I am surprised by that fact. But it is, as best I can judge, a fact.

On February 11, 2004, I directly challenged Greenspan on his power.

RON PAUL: Frederick Hayek was fond of saying that the managed economy was in danger because it was based on a pretense of knowledge, that certain things the economic planners don't know and, for instance, he would agree with me that we don't know, you don't know, the Congress doesn't know what the overnight rates ought to be, yet we reject the marketplace. But it is part of the system. And I understand that. But doesn't it ever occur to you that maybe there is too much power in the hands of those who control monetary policy, the power to create the financial bubbles, the power to maybe bring the bubble about, the power to change the value of the stock market within minutes? That to me is just an ominous power and challenges the whole concept of freedom and liberty and sound money.

ALAN GREENSPAN: Congressman, as I have said to you before, the problem you are alluding to is the conversion of a commodity standard to fiat money. We have statutorily gone onto a fiat money standard, and as a consequence of that it is inevitable that the authority, which is the producer of the money supply, will have inordinate power. And that is one of the reasons why I have indicated because of that, and because of the fact that we are unelected officials, it is mandatory that we be as transparent as we conceivably can, and remember that we are accountable to the electorate and to the Congress. And the power that we have is all granted by you. We don't have any capability whatsoever to do anything without the agreement or even the acquiescence of the Congress of the United States. We recognize that and one of the reasons I am here today is to endeavor to convey why we are doing what we are doing. And I will continue to do that, and I am sure that all of my colleagues are fully aware of the responsibility that the Congress has given us, and I trust that we adhere to the principles of the Constitution of the United States more so than one would ordinarily do.

Greenspan's last appearance before the Financial Services Committee occurred on July 20, 2005. On this occasion, I pressed him hard about what kind of conditions would require him to reconsider the use of gold in the monetary system. Prefacing the question, I pointed out that central banks still hold gold, evidently on the belief that it does represent a monetary purpose. They hold no other commodities, and even though they have been selling gold over the years, there's still a lot of gold held by the International Monetary Fund and the central banks.

RON PAUL: Even you, in the 1960s, described the paper system as a scheme for the confiscation of wealth. . . . Is it not true that the paper system that we work with today is actually a scheme to default on our debt? And is it not true that, for this reason, that's a good argument for people not—eventually, at some day—wanting to buy Treasury bills because they will be paid back with cheaper dollars? . . .

And aligned with this question, I would like to ask something dealing exactly with gold. . . . If paper money—today it seems to be working rather well—but if the paper system doesn't work, when will the time come? What will the signs be that we should reconsider gold?

ALAN GREENSPAN: Well, you say central banks own gold—or monetary authorities own gold. The United States is a large gold holder. And you have to ask yourself: Why do we hold gold? And the answer is essentially, implicitly, the one that you've raised—namely that, over the generations, when fiat monies arose and, indeed, created the type of problems—which I think you correctly identify—of the 1970s, although the implication that it was some scheme or conspiracy gives it a much more conscious focus than actually, as I recall, it was occurring. It was more inadvertence that created the basic problems.

But as I've testified here before to a similar question, central bankers began to realize in the late 1970s how deleterious a factor the inflation was. And, indeed, since the late 70s central bankers generally have behaved as though we were on the gold standard. And, indeed, the extent of liquidity contraction that has occurred as a consequence of the various different efforts on the part of the monetary authorities is a clear indication that we recognize that excess of credit of liquidity creates inflation which, in turn, undermines economic growth. So that the question is: Would there be any advantage, at this particular stage, in going back to the gold standard? And the answer is: I don't think so, because we're acting as though we were there. Would it have been a question at least open in 1971, as you put it? And the answer is yes. Remember, the gold price was $800 an ounce. We were dealing with extraordinary imbalances, interest rates were up sharply, the system looked to be highly unstable and we needed to do something, and we did something. Paul Volcker, as you may recall, in 1979 came into office and put a very severe clamp on the expansion on credit. And that led to a long sequence of events here, which we are benefiting from up to this date.

So I think central banking, I believe, has learned the dangers of fiat money and I think as a consequence of that we've behaved as though there are, indeed, real reserves underneath this system.

So it looks like it will take high consumer price and producer price inflation for Greenspan ever to give token reconsideration to gold. In the meantime, I believe, many central banks of the world as well as the IMF will hold on to gold. What we are seeing is that the Western banks, the nations that have lived beyond their means, are selling gold at the same time the more growth-oriented countries in the East are buying gold.

As for his claim that central bankers were behaving as if on a gold standard, the record of the 1990s indicates otherwise, and the result is the catastrophe that began in 2008.

The message Greenspan was delivering in 1966 was quite different from his message and policy as Federal Reserve Board chairman. In one private conversation, he did acknowledge his association with Murray Rothbard but volunteered no value judgment. Maybe Rothbard had been a favorable influence on Greenspan, since it was during that time that the excellent article on gold and freedom was written.

In a way, it's pretty astounding. After inflating the currency endlessly for every correction and every political crisis during his tenure, he claimed that he recognized the danger of how excessive credit of liquidity creates inflation. Now in the middle of possibly the greatest correction of credit creation of all history, Greenspan remains in denial as to his most significant contribution to the crisis. I would say that he never came close to achieving what he claimed—that he could get paper to substitute for gold when managed by wise central bankers. History will prove that goal is unachievable, and any sophistication in managing fiat currency may well delay corrections, but in doing so only allows a greater financial bubble to form. That's what today's crisis is all about.

Many libertarians had actually advanced the theory that Greenspan was still a true believer and would advance the cause of sound money and freedom when appropriate. I never thought that a possibility, and as time moved on, I became more firmly convinced that pragmatism, a philosophic position Ayn Rand hated, drove Greenspan. He visited the House Committee on Oversight and Reform on October 24, 2008, and was welcomed as a "distinguished" former Federal Reserve Board chairman.

This was the final word on Greenspan.

Most of his testimony was designed as an attempt to protect his reputation and to explain away his shortcomings as Federal Reserve Board chairman. His testimony was pathetic. He made the point that the computer programs that they were using to anticipate these problems were not well designed. The only reason there was an expansion of debt is there was an excessive demand for our debt; it was not a consequence of Federal Reserve Board policy. And to climax his arguments, he said that he did make a mistake, that indeed we did not have enough regulations on the market. In other words, create the conditions for malinvestment and compensate for them by having more government regulations. As the hearings were coming to a close, I could only conclude: Greenspan is not John Galt.

History will show that Greenspan, during his years as Fed chairman (1987–2006), planted all the seeds of the financial calamity that erupted in 2007 and 2008. For the same reason a disease cannot be cured by more of the germ that caused it, the inflation and debt accumulation of the Obama years will not inflate our way out of it. This depression will likely last and last. If the depression lasts a decade or more, its length cannot be blamed solely on Greenspan. That blame will be placed on the current Federal Reserve Board, Congress, the President, the Treasury, but above all on Keynesian economic policy, the same philosophy that gave us the Great Depression of the 1930s.

The economic downturn is the necessary correction of the artificial boom period produced by the central bank's easy credit and artificially low interest rates. The duration itself is a consequence of the interference with the liquidation of debt and malinvestment and adjustment in prices of labor, goods, and services. It's too much to ask politicians or bureaucrats *not* to centrally plan the economy, especially when the market is struggling to rectify all the mistakes that come as a consequence of the Federal Reserve Board policy.

CHAPTER 7

CONVERSATIONS WITH BERNANKE

I've since had several run-ins with Ben Bernanke. In fact, I've grilled him continually at every meeting of the Financial Services Committee, so that at least I know that he has heard another view. He became chairman on February 1, 2006. In an exchange with him on July 20 of that year, I questioned him in detail on the secrecy of the "plunge protection team"—the Working Group on Financial Markets that included the secretary of the Treasury and the chairmen of the Federal Reserve Board, the Securities and Exchange Commission, and the Commodity Futures Trading Commission—on some existing biases against economic growth, and the role of the Fed in the event of financial crisis.

Here is how the exchange went.

RON PAUL: I have a question dealing with the Working Group on Financial Markets. I want to learn more about that group and actually what authority they have and what they do. Could you tell me, as a member of that group, how often they meet and how often they take action; and have they done something recently? And are there reports sent out by this particular group?

BEN BERNANKE: Yes, Congressman. The President's Working Group was convened by the President, I believe, after the 1987 stock market crash. It meets irregularly, I would guess about four or five times a year, but I am not exactly sure. And its primary function is advisory, to prepare reports. I mentioned earlier that we have been asked to prepare a report on the terrorism risk insurance. So that is what we generally do.

RON PAUL: In the media you will find articles that will claim that it is a lot more than an advisory group, you know, if there is a stock market crash, that you literally have a lot of authority, you know, to impose restrictions on the market. And we are talking about many trillions of dollars slushing around in all the financial markets, and this involves Treasury and, of course, the Fed, as well as the SEC and the CFTC. So there is a lot of potential there.

And the reason this came to my attention was just recently there was an article that actually made a charge that out of this group came actions to interfere with the prices of General Motors stock. Have you read that, or do you know anything about that?

BEN BERNANKE: No, sir, I don't.

RON PAUL: Because they were charging that there was a problem with General Motors, and then there was a spike in GM's stock prices. But back to the issue of the meeting. You tell me it meets irregularly, but there are minutes kept, or are there reports made on this group?

BEN BERNANKE: I believe there are records kept by the staff. These are staff mostly from Treasury, but also from the other agencies.

RON PAUL: And they would be available to us in the committee?

BEN BERNANKE: I don't know. I am sorry, I don't know.

RON PAUL: The other question I have deals with a comment made by one of the members of the Federal Reserve Board just recently. He made a statement which was a rather common statement made. He expressed a relief that the economy was weakening, mainly inferring that the weakening economy would help contain inflation. And I hear these comments a lot of times, the economy is too strong, and therefore we need a weaker economy. If this assumption is correct—would you agree that this assumption, that a weaker economy is helpful when you are worried about inflation?

BEN BERNANKE: Congressman, as I talked about in my testimony, we need to go to a sustainable pace. We need to have a pace which matches the underlying productive capacity; that will probably be a bit less robust than the last few years, because over the last few years we were also reemploying underutilized resources, and going forward we don't have that slack to put to work.

RON PAUL: But if you accept the principle, as it seemed to be in this quote, that if you are worried about inflation, you slow up the economy, and then inflation is brought down, it is lessened, it infers that inflation is caused by economic growth, and I don't happen to accept that, because most people accept the fact that inflation is really a monetary phenomenon. And it also introduces the notion that growth is bad, and yet I see growth as good. Whether it is three or four or five or six, if you don't have monetary inflation, we don't need to worry, because if you have good growth in the marketplace rather than artificial growth, that it is this growth that causes your productivity to increase. You have an increase in productivity, and it does help bring prices down, but it doesn't deal with inflation.

And I think what I am talking about here could relate to the concerns of the gentleman from Massachusetts about real wages. There is a lot of concern about real wages versus nominal wages, but I think it is a characteristic of an economy that is based on fiat currency that is just losing its value that it is inevitable that the real labor goes down. As a matter of fact, Keynes advocated it. He realized that in a slump, that real wages had to go down; and he believed that you could get real wages down by inflation, that the nominal wage doesn't come on and keep the nominal wage up, have the real wage come down and sort of deceive the working man. But it really doesn't work because ultimately the working man knows he is losing, and he demands cost of living increases.

So could you help me out in trying to understand why we should ever attack economic growth? Why can't we just say economic growth is good and it helps lower prices because it increases productivity?

BEN BERNANKE: Congressman, I agree with you. Growth doesn't cause inflation; what causes inflation is monetary conditions or financial conditions that stimulate spending which grows more quickly than the underlying capacity of the economy to produce. Anything that increases the economy to produce, be it greater productivity, greater workforce, other factors that are productive, is only positive. It reduces inflation.

RON PAUL: Do you see our deficits that we produce—and that you have control on—as a burden to the Fed in managing monetary affairs and maintaining interest rates as well as maybe even living with a lower increase in the money supply?

BEN BERNANKE: Well, in our short-term monetary policymaking, we are able to adjust for the conditions of fiscal policy, however they may be. I think fiscal issues are more important in the long-term sense because of the long-term obligations we have, for example, for entitlements. We have not found the fiscal situation to be a major impediment to our short-term management of monetary policy.

I suspected that Bernanke was a bit nervous during that exchange, and was unnecessarily close-lipped about issues about which he was surely well informed. He also struck me as taken aback to be dealing with such technical topics in public, and struggled to get beyond clichés about sustained paces and the like. Finally, he concluded in a way that we expect from a lifelong devotee of monetary expansion: no matter how bad the fiscal situation gets, nothing will serve as an impediment to the Fed.

Here is a telling exchange from July 18, 2007, in which I attempt to warn him that the current policy is not sustainable, that a crisis is coming.

> RON PAUL: I find it rather ironic that the Federal Reserve has complete control over the money supply but yet it is the Treasury that is supposed to protect the value of the dollar. It seems like you have a little bit of responsibility for the value of the dollar as well.
>
> I have a question about the GDP. In the first quarter, our GDP didn't do so well. It was less than 1 percent [annualized]. Our population growth average is about 1.5 percent. So, if we have total wealth divided by the population, we actually have negative growth. Could this not be part of the explanation on why some people feel inequality; that they're not doing as well in the economy? Wouldn't this explain some of the concerns that we have?
>
> BEN BERNANKE: Congressman, that was of course a single quarter and there were a number of temporary factors that held down GDP growth in the first quarter including liquidation of the inventory overhang (which I mentioned before), a swing in our trade balance (a temporary swing), and a temporary decline in federal defense spending. All of those things have been reversing now, and so I think we will be seeing in the second

quarter something closer to 3 percent growth. Between the first half of the year, overall, it will show a more healthy rate of growth.

RON PAUL: We have a savings rate which is negative. If we had true capitalism, this would be very, very serious because we'd have no savings and no capital to invest. Today, with our monetary system, we resort to other means. We can create credit and money out of thin air and it acts as capital by stealing value from the existing currency. We've been doing that for a long time, so the process can continue but it literally is the inflation.

Also, we can resort to borrowing overseas and we are permitted because we have the reserve currency of the world to export our inflation and that seems to be a free ride for us as well. But, how long can we fool the world? How long can we continue with a current account deficit of 6 percent if our productive jobs are going overseas? And, like the gentleman mentioned before about more jobs going overseas, eventually, this is going to catch up with us. Is it conceivable that we could live on capital formation by creation of money and credit out of thin air? If that's the case, we wouldn't ever have to go to work again if that's true. It seems like we really have to go to work; we really have to save; we really have to invest; and we really have to get these jobs back.

But I really see so many of our problems as a consequence of a monetary system that discourages savings, encourages a free ride for us because there is still a lot of trust for the dollar (although that trust is going down every day), and I think we have to face up to the consequences of what this might mean to us.

BEN BERNANKE: First, our national saving includes corporate saving as well as household saving. If you put those together, you get a positive number, so there is some net saving going on in the United States. But, Congressman, you're absolutely right that we're also relying pretty heavily on borrowing from abroad which is our current account deficit. I think that's sustainable for a while because foreigners seem quite interested in acquiring U.S. assets. We have very deep and liquid financial markets.

However, I also agree with you that that's not a long-term, sustainable situation by any means and we need to be working to try to bring that current account deficit down over time. In the answer to a previous question I talked a bit about the importance of structural change: increase the savings here in the United States, increasing attention to domestic demand with our trading partners.

RON PAUL: You did say in your talk that the predominant policy concern was inflation, which is encouraging that there is a concern. Of course, once again, inflation is a monetary phenomenon and we have to deal with it.

War, sometimes, is not healthy for a currency or for keeping prices down, at least inflation. It's hard to find, in all of history, when war didn't create price inflation because, even in ancient times, countries resorted to clipping coins and diluting values or whatever. They inflated the currency because people generally don't like to pay for the war. And yet, in the seventies, we had consequences of guns and butter. Now, we're having guns and butter again (we're having consequences) and it just looks like we may well come to a '79–'80. Do you anticipate that there is a possibility that we'll face a crisis of the dollar such as we had in '79 and 1980?

BEN BERNANKE: The Federal Reserve is committed to maintaining low and stable inflation and I'm very confident that we'll be able to do that.

RON PAUL: You're not answering whether or not you anticipate a problem.

BEN BERNANKE: I'm not anticipating a problem like '79–'80.

RON PAUL: With your fingers crossed, I guess. Okay. Thank you.

Apparently, the finger crossing didn't work. Several times in the above exchange, Bernanke says that he expects a bright future of a growing economy with no apparent problems on the way. Keep in mind that this was two weeks before the collapse of the Bear Stearns hedge funds, and one year ahead of the wholesale crumbling of the American financial system. All problems, he says, will be cured about our liquid financial markets. Why anyone takes his view seriously today is a mystery. Finally, he confesses his belief that government spending is a source of economic growth, a superstition of the old-line Keynesians that you can rob some people and give to other people and somehow magically create prosperity.

Later that year, November 8, 2007, we had another con-
frontation. This time I specifically questioned him on the
housing bubble.

RON PAUL: The best way I could describe the problems
that we face here in this country, as well as the problem
that the Federal Reserve faces, is that we're indeed between the rock and the hard place, because we have a
serious problem. We don't talk much about how we got
here; we talk about how we're going to patch it up.

The bubble has been burst. We saw what happened
after the NASDAQ bubble burst. We don't ask how
it was created.

And then we have a housing bubble, and it's deflating and then spreading. And yet nobody says, where
does it come from?

And what is the advice that you generally get, and
that is, inflate the currency. They don't say inflate the
currency, they don't say debase the currency, they
don't say devalue the currency, they don't say cheat
the people. They say lower the interest rates.

But they never ask you, and I don't hear you say too
often, the only way I can lower interest rates is I have
to create more money. I have to lower the discount
rate, I have to make it generous, I have to increase
reserves, I have to lower the interest rates and fix the
interest rates—overnight rates.

And the only way you can do this is by increasing
the money supply. And I see this as the problem that
we don't want to talk about.

Currently, of course, we can't follow the money supply with M3 but we can follow one of your statistics, which is the MZM—the ready cash available—and we see that inflation is alive and well. That money supply figure is going up about 20 percent, annualized.

And this just means that the dollar gets weaker. And everybody says, well, the dollar is [weaker]—that's great. Dollar weaker, we're going to have exports. And that is a fallacy—maybe for a month or two, but it just invites inflation.

And unless we get down to the bottom of it and define what inflation is and not look at only prices—this was talked about by the free-market economists all through the twentieth century. They said, Beware: they will increase their money supply, but they will make you concentrate on prices. And they will give you CPIs and PPIs and, you know, fudge those figures and they'll talk about wage and price controls to solve our problems.

And we ignored the fundamental flaw, and that is that not only have we had a subprime market in housing; the whole economic system is subprime, in that we have artificially low interest rates. And it wasn't under your tenure in office; it's been going on for ten years and longer and now we're bearing the fruits of that policy.

I mean, a 1 percent interest rate, overnight rates and that's not a distortion? Instead of looking at these—the consumer prices, which nobody in this country really believes, we need to talk about the distortion, the malinvestment, the misdirection, the bad information that is gotten from artificially low interest rates.

In many ways, some people refer to you as a price fixer, you know, because you fix interest rates.

The market is powerful, and usually overwhelms and does come into play, but when the Fed fixes an interest rate at 1 percent, that is price-fixing.

At the end of your testimony, you suggested that we should address this housing crisis, and we should have rules that would address deceptive lending practices. And I just think that is not the answer at all.

The real deception is when we distort the value of money, when we create money out of thin air. We have no savings. Yet there's so-called capital. There's money available. But it comes from what you have to do and the pressures put on you. So I think we have to get back to the very fundamentals of where this problem comes from. And the bubbles occur when we have this malinvestment and the creation of new money.

So my question boils down to this. How in the world can we expect to solve the problems of inflation, that is, the increase in the supply of money, with more inflation?

BEN BERNANKE: Well, Congressman, first, just a small technical point. On the growth in money, money growth has been pretty moderate over the last few years. The increase in MZM is probably related to the financial turmoil. People have been taking their savings out of, you know, risky assets, putting them into the bank, and that makes the money data show faster growth.

So I'm not sure that's indicative of policy, necessarily.

What we're trying to do is follow the mandate that Congress gave us. And the mandate that Congress gave us is to look at employment and inflation as measured by domestic price growth.

And as I talked about today, and I think you would agree that we do see risks to inflation and we are taking those into account and we want to make sure that prices remain as stable as possible in the United States.

RON PAUL: How can you do this and pursue this—the policy that you have—without further weakening the dollar? There's a dollar crisis out there and people's money is being stolen; people who have saved, they're being robbed. I mean, if you have a devaluation of the dollar at 10 percent, people have been robbed of 10 percent. But how can you pursue this policy without addressing the subject that somebody's losing their wealth because of a weaker dollar? And it's going to lead to higher interest rates and a weaker economy.

BEN BERNANKE: If somebody has their wealth in dollars and they're going to buy consumer goods in dollars— it's a typical American—then the decline in the dollar, the only effect it has on their buying powers, it makes imported goods more expensive.

RON PAUL: Yes, but not if you're retired and elderly and you have CDs and their cost of living is going up no matter what your CPI says. Their cost of living is going up and they are hurting. And that's why the people in this country are very upset.

Now, that was the last time we had an exchange before the meltdown. Bernanke was more evasive than ever before. He didn't address any of the specifics. Moreover, he displayed not the slightest concern about an impending problem. I suspect that I could have questioned him all day and received only more bromides in response. What he knew in his heart is another matter. That day he was in full propaganda mode.

An exchange on March 24, 2009, long after the crisis began, ran as follows.

RON PAUL: Do you operate with the idea that capitalism failed and they need us more than ever before to solve these problems? Or do you say, "No, there is some truth to this. As a matter of fact, a lot of truth to it is that we brought this upon ourselves, that we had too much government, too much interference in interest rates, too much risk, moral risk, built into the system."

Because if you come from the viewpoint that says that the market does not work, I can understand everything you do. But if I see that you totally rejected the market, and that we have to do something about it, I can understand why we in the Congress, and you in Treasury, and you in the Fed continue to do this.

So where do you put the blame, on the market or on crony capitalism that we've been living with probably for three decades?

BEN BERNANKE: Congressman, I certainly do not reject capitalism. I don't think this is a failure of capitalism per se, and I also think that free markets should be the primary mechanism for allocating capital. They've shown over many decades that they can allocate money to new enterprises, to new technologies very effectively, and so we want to maintain that free capital market structure.

It is nevertheless the case that we've seen over the decades, in the centuries, that financial systems can be prone to panics, runs, booms, busts, and, for better or worse, we have developed mechanisms like deposit insurance and lender of last resort to avert those things. Those protections in turn require some oversight to avoid the buildup of risks.

RON PAUL: May I interrupt, please?

BEN BERNANKE: Certainly.

RON PAUL: Isn't that what creates the moral hazard, though? Isn't that the problem rather than the solution?

BEN BERNANKE: Well, we had the reason the Fed was created in 1913 was because in 1907 and in 1914, there were big financial panics and there was no regulation there and people thought that was a big problem, back in the nineteenth century as well.

There is something fishy about the head of the world's most powerful government bureaucracy, one that is involved in a full-time counterfeiting operation to sustain monopolistic financial cartels, and the world's most powerful central planner who sets the price of money worldwide, proclaiming the glories of capitalism. Even when faced with the dreadful consequences of the hazards created by his own institution, he refused to face reality, or at least refused to admit it.

I recall seeing Bernanke with a bit of a smile on his face when I suggested my solution would not be listened to since that would make all the important players involved in spending trillions of dollars irrelevant. That is one thing they are not interested in: irrelevancy. Politicians must justify their existence in managing the affairs of state. They first create the problems and then they are delighted with all the activity in expanding government and solving the very problems they created.

What none of them will admit is that the market is more powerful than the central banks and all the economic planners put together. Although it may take time, the market always wins. Sometimes the market is forced to go underground to achieve the activity needed for human survival. That day may be fast approaching.

Some people have been surprised by Bernanke's irresponsible conduct of monetary policy. There was no reason to be surprised. He was on record promising unlimited amounts of inflation should the need arise. If Greenspan was cocky about the genius of central bankers, Bernanke is even more so.

His comment to Milton Friedman at a dinner honoring Professor Friedman's ninetieth birthday on November 8, 2002, reveals it all. He apologized to Professor Friedman and said Friedman was absolutely right—the Depression was the fault of the Federal Reserve. It wasn't the fault of the central bank managing a fiat currency or participating in credit expansion or debt monetization; the problem lay only with the Federal Reserve's inability or unwillingness to inflate the currency early and massively starting in 1929.

Bernanke closed his remarks by directly addressing Friedman: "You're right, we did it. We're very sorry. But thanks to you, we won't do it again."

The fault indeed does lie with the Federal Reserve—but obviously for opposite reasons. It was the credit expansion of the 1920s causing the stock market bubble that was the real cause of the crash. The crash was then compounded by the necessary corrections being interfered with by both Hoover and FDR and the concurrent Congresses.

Bernanke may be serious and believe he can prevent the consequences of the Fed's mistakes of the past several decades. But he is wrong. He may dampen the market's enthusiasm for deflation, but the pain and suffering from the "unlimited expansion of credit" that a much younger Greenspan warned us about will still come. Emphatically, Greenspan said there was "no way" to protect savings from confiscation through inflation.

So even if Bernanke can head off actual deflation, which he sees as our only threat, the stability of the financial system cannot be restored by massive expansion of money and credit under the fiat dollar reserve financial system.

Here lies the crux of the problem. If Bernanke and his friends argue that the Fed was at fault, and all the Austrian school economists agree as well that the Fed was the cause of the Depression, to solve the crisis it must be resolved as to exactly how it happened. Was it too much credit expansion or not enough? That is the question.

Those who place their faith in paper say "pour it on"; the dangers can be avoided and the problems solved. Those who use reason can quickly understand that noninflationary commodity money is the only answer possible to the endless boom-bust cycles.

Even dropping money from helicopters, as Bernanke once advised, if it ever became necessary, will guarantee that the dollar will be destroyed as so many other currencies throughout history have been. Just remember, dropping paper money from helicopters will just result in the money being blown away.

What did Milton Friedman believe about money? He was a free-market economist who called himself a libertarian and contributed tremendously to an understanding of how the free market works. There was, however, strong disagreement between Milton Friedman and the hard-money camp of the Austrian school. Friedman believed that the money supply needed to expand in order to support economic growth. He despaired, from time to time, of the Fed's incentive to do what was right, but he believed in the old monetarist principle that the money supply needed to expand by some amount.

On occasion in the early 1980s, I debated Dr. Friedman on this issue. He was always courteous and many times complimentary toward my efforts. For a time in the early 1980s, I did a TV interview show for my congressional district and he appeared as a guest on that show. In 1996, when I reentered politics and was running for Congress, I talked to him and asked him if he would write a letter for me in support of the campaign, making the point that economic liberty and personal liberty were one and the same. I was running in a very conservative Bible-belt district, yet I took some civil libertarian positions that were challenging to many. He wrote a delightful little note explaining that these freedoms were one and the same and implied strongly that if you want personal liberty in your religious affairs and your home schooling affairs, you should endorse personal liberty across the board as well as economic liberty.

The Friedman quote I used in my campaign stated:

> We very badly need to have more Representatives in the House who understand in a principled way the importance of property rights and religious freedom for the preservation and extension of human freedom in general ... I wish you every success.

I sometimes wonder if Friedman, when witnessing what Greenspan and Bernanke have done, might have come around. After all, Anna Schwartz, his coauthor on his history of monetary policy in the United States has been commenting freely on the pages of the *Wall Street Journal*: "There never would have been a sub-prime mortgage crisis if the Fed had been alert. This is something Alan Greenspan must answer for." Further: "In general, it's easier for a central bank to be accommodative, to be loose, to be promoting conditions that make everybody feel that things are going well."

CHAPTER 8

CONGRESS'S INTEREST IN MONETARY POLICY

I have for years sensed a total disinterest in monetary policy by members of Congress as well as members of the Financial Services Committee. An incident confirmed this skepticism. After I had brought up the subject of gold in a Financial Services hearing, in all seriousness, a member asked me in private whether the dollar was "backed" by gold, having up until then assumed that it was. I don't think this is unusual. Many of the people who are supposedly in charge of monitoring the system are surprisingly ignorant about even the most basic aspects of how the system works.

There has been little understanding of any economic policy in Washington. The idea that the government and the Fed should be completely out of the business of central economic planning is not even seen as worthy of discussion. And yet it is Congress that is put in an oversight role. It should exercise that role. But that means doing the work necessary to learn about the topic, and not merely deferring to the big shots in charge of the bureaucracies Congress supposedly oversees.

Most members of Congress are not automatically hostile to

gold or even to the abolition of the Fed. Their attitude is more one of surprise that anybody would even consider it. At the same time, I've never heard a member express support for paper money on grounds that it facilitates the expansion of the state. Most don't see the connection at all. They aren't even curious about the topic.

What the Fed and paper money have done for Congress is lead legislators to believe that there are no limits on what they can spend, on what they can propose, and what they can accomplish. They really do behave like college students on spring break who are using their parents' credit cards with no limit. They don't think about the money. They don't think about who or what is paying the bills. The ability to do what they want is just taken for granted. They aren't even interested in looking at the accounting books. But they would hit the roof if the card were ever declined.

The point is, unless one has a strong love of liberty, ignorance regarding money is not something that most members of Congress regret. This ignorance is what allows conservatives and liberals alike to spend, borrow, tax, and inflate to finance their various programs, both foreign and domestic.

There is also the serious matter of the manner in which the Fed intervenes in politics, not just every once in a while but constantly. A famous example of this took place when Arthur Burns was chairman of the Fed (1970–1978). He tightened up on secrecy during his reign and ended the practice of keeping verbatim minutes during Federal Open Market Committee meetings. His intervention in politics is indisputable. Following the election of Jimmy Carter in 1976, he dearly wanted to be reappointed. He cut the discount rate and accelerated money growth. True, he was a Republican, but he wanted to go down in history as bipartisan.

A memo from a staff aide, reported by William Greider, informed Burns that "Carter can be seduced . . . reappointment would make Carter out to be a high-minded statesman. . . . Carter will have to be assured that, if you are reappointed, you will not continue to publicly criticize everything that is near and dear to him."[1]

Sadly for Burns, the courtship failed. Even more sadly for the country, the courtship wrecked the dollar further. It also wrecked the Carter presidency, as he dealt with the worst bout of price inflation in more than a century. Finally, the inflation backfired even against the Democrats and brought Ronald Reagan to power. Such is the lagging effect of shortsighted efforts to manipulate the political environment to benefit particular Fed governors and banking interests. Despite his sympathy for the gold standard, Reagan did nothing about the issue. His advisers successfully kept him quiet on this issue, fearing that he would be seen as crazy or kooky. Similarly, many people in Congress were privately sympathetic but not knowledgeable enough to take up the cause.

In the meantime, the Fed's involvement in the "political business cycle" is a well-documented fact. The Fed tends to loosen before elections and is far more likely to tolerate downturns between presidential elections and Fed appointments. This is an open secret in Washington. We all pretend that the Fed is not a political operation, and yet everyone

---

1. William Greider, *Secrets of the Temple* (New York: Simon & Schuster, 1987), p. 346.

knows that it is among the most political institutions in the entire government.

As the years rolled on, it became more apparent to me that the leadership for a return to sound money would never come from the U.S. Congress. Of course, Congress could abolish the Fed tomorrow if it wanted to. The representatives' ignorance of economics, as well as the benefits they enjoy from irresponsible spending, prevent this. Our leaders will only respond when the people of this country rise up and demand honesty in money.

Of course, not every supporter of the Fed is somehow a participant in a conspiracy to control the world. Everyone who wants to control the world, however, whether for the benefits of gaining wealth or power, must have control of the monetary system. It's been that way throughout history. The greater the degree of freedom the people enjoy, the sounder has been the money. Tyranny always goes hand in hand with government's wrecking of the money system.

The problem is not only a lust for power; ironically, benevolence and humanitarianism drive many to seek power over others. They believe for humanitarian reasons that the strong and wise have an obligation to subject the weak and ignorant to the whims of government control. As they gain more influence and power, they become more convinced that they are saviors of mankind, and if any resistance or obstacles appear that limit their power, they believe that brute force must be used to impose their "goodwill" on the stubborn few. The purpose of freedom vanishes from their minds.

The French Jacobins in the eighteenth century were so convinced that their cause was right that even using the guillotine to enforce their will on others for their alleged own good was legitimate. Some who promoted the Iraq War were motivated in the same manner. They rationalized a humanitarian excuse for the war even as more than 4,000 Americans died and tens of thousands were wounded. The one million Iraqis who died, and hundreds of thousands who were injured, and the millions of refugees were all justified because of the "goodness" the instigators of the war brought to the world.

No matter the true reason for wanting to control others, the tax and borrowing system never suffices. Control of money by government and central banking is always required.

As long as there is wealth available, the people will not complain about the takeover of the monetary system. The day the Fed came into being in 1913 may have been the beginning of the end, but the powers it obtained and the mischief it caused took a long time to become a serious issue and a concern for average Americans.

But now our wealth is drained. Our productivity is sharply diminished. Our freedoms are eroded. Our empire is fragile.

And the scheme that long ago eventually gave us the Federal Reserve Act of 1913 is being challenged. The Fed's inability to manage this admittedly unworkable system is more apparent every day. The question remains whether a new conspiracy on money and central banking can replace what we have, or will we choose a system of money compatible with a free society?

The answer will come from an informed and enraged populace. Congress will then respond, but only when it is impossible not to.

There is another force that cannot be ignored: the market. It can overrule even the power of central bankers and government agencies. If nothing else, once the system brought on by the central banks becomes dysfunctional, the underground (real) economy always grows. It existed in the Soviet system as well.

I recall a fascinating trip during my days as an Air Force flight surgeon. After visiting Portugal, Italy, Greece, and Ethiopia, we stopped in Turkey and Iran and then went on to Pakistan, checking up on the outposts of our empire. The senior officers located at a base near Peshawar, Pakistan, took our crew up to the Khyber Pass for a shopping trip at the Afghan border—an area that is now likely serving as the home of our current nemesis, Osama bin Laden. I remember that as we traveled through the desolate, rugged mountains the commander explained to me that, despite the lack of apparent activity, plenty of tribal natives were present in the region.

When we got to the border, we could not enter Afghanistan, which, at the time, was allied with the Soviets. But nearby there was a place of great importance where East met West. It was a huge cave set up as an exchange post with goods as numerous as a giant department store's. Russian and Eastern goods were sold, as well as American and other Western goods. It was peaceful and rather quiet under the earth. Here the people were permitted to trade and converse (authorities on both sides knew of the underground market because it served the interests of both), while up above, the Cold War raged.

Governments and central banks mess things up, but the market, if it is permitted to operate, is capable of sorting out the mess even under duress. There will always be the underground, smugglers, and the black market, as long as we allow

our governments to plunder and control us by making voluntary exchanges and associations illegal. It is government controls themselves that give rise to a black market. By destroying
money and fueling the growth of the state, the institution of a
central bank is the biggest generator of underground criminal
activity ever.

Some of our political allies charge that the powerful elites
who run things and are found repeatedly in the Fed, the Treasury, and the presidency, plan and purposely cause certain
events like 9/11 and our current financial crisis. I don't believe
that. But I do believe that many members of the elite make
the best they can out of certain events because they facilitate
their efforts to achieve their goals. Rahm Emanuel, Obama's
chief of staff, said recently: "You never want a serious crisis to
go to waste." Obama concurred with Emanuel's assessment.

Whereas I see today's crisis as a reason to make an argument for liberty and sound money, others use it to further
expand the size and scope of government. Physical or economic fears cause many people to succumb to the offer of authoritarians to protect them at all costs. Many of the laws
passed after 9/11 had already been proposed prior to the event,
but rejected. Economic planners have many plans to socialize
our economy and globalize the effort, if only the popular sen-
timent will accept it. And why? Socialization always and
everywhere means more power to the state, more control to
bureaucrats, more security for the elites, and always at the expense of the rest of us. Economic chaos assists in this effort.

But to purposely bring on catastrophic economic events such
as the current situation would be a bad move for anyone, because this level of calamity can pose danger even to the insiders.

Wealth loss by deflation and inflation can affect everyone. Political chaos is not always beneficial to those in charge and may in fact be a danger to them. However, they will not hesitate for a minute to do whatever they think is necessary to maintain and expand their control. The insiders who work so hard to undermine sound money to serve their own interests are the same ones who are quite capable of accumulating gold as an ultimate protection against the economic chaos they created.

Blowback, whether from a seriously flawed foreign policy or from a ridiculously flawed economic and monetary policy, comes as a surprise to many of the designers of this policy because of their own naive belief that they are all-wise. They believe they can always manage conditions that will pacify the people and secure their own economic and political power. But events like Vietnam, the Iraq War, 9/11, or the current economic crisis unify many average citizens against the power elites. The political insiders would just as soon not encourage a rebellion. That is not to say they oppose wars like Vietnam and Iraq, but the popular outcry after it's become known that the wars were fought on false pretenses and have gone badly wrong is something they would prefer not to have to deal with. A "small" 9/11 they can manage, but not a huge one.

In any case, I believe that concentrating too much on the Fed "conspiracy," one that works hand in hand with Congress, gives the system more credit or blame than it deserves and distracts from the more important issue of bad ideology. Authoritarianism, supporting statism on moral grounds for whatever reason, is the real threat.

These secret powers that the Fed and Treasury have usurped from Congress are the source of much evil. Let me be clear and realistic: elimination of the Fed—and the Exchange Stabilization Fund and all the other powers that go with it—will most likely not occur before the dollar crisis hits. In the meantime, due to the economic downturn we're witnessing, a coalition of principled people across the political spectrum may well be able to force Congress to exert more oversight. The American people deserve the information.

Better political decisions will be made when more people and members of Congress understand how all these backroom deals by the Federal Reserve only serve the interests of the elite and destroy the economy that average Americans depend on. Getting rid of the Fed will end the ability to control the people through monopoly on money and banking. While I do not endorse the views of people who write of the conspiracy to control the world through the Fed, I understand what it is that motivates such concerns. Central banks and their shenanigans fuel a kind of public paranoia that is not entirely based on myth. Getting rid of the Fed would help restore confidence in the system.

CHAPTER 9

THE CURRENT MESS

In 2008, a shock hit the American people. The economy had been in the doldrums for some time, but in the fall, the house of cards really began to tumble. Government panicked and the American people woke up to the reality that they had been living in a bubble economy that was now completely popping. Government flew into action with the idea that it could stop the problem from getting worse and put us on the road to recovery. But after trillions spent, and unprecedented levels of intervention, the problems have only grown worse, contrary to all the promises of the political class.

Many accusations were made about who was responsible for the downturn. It was argued, and still is, that it's a reflection of the shortcomings of free-market capitalism. Some say it is solely the result of not enough regulations by the banking authorities, especially of the derivatives market. Others suggest that consumers' lack of enthusiasm to spend is to blame. Others say that all problems would be solved if banks would lend more—as if adding more poison to a poisoned patient amounts to a cure.

Then-Secretary of the Treasury Henry Paulson simplified it by saying that the downturn in the housing market has caused all the trouble. He and others concluded that the government should stimulate new housing and do whatever's possible to keep the prices of houses from falling. They contended that since house values were dropping, the mortgages and the many derivatives associated with securitization had become illiquid, and bailing out this market would reverse the deflationary process.

But—and this is crucial—focusing on the housing market alone was just the last in a parade of claims about the root problem. There are other sectors that have suffered, in finance, car manufacturing, services, retails, and stocks. These are all merely symptoms of a deeper problem: the Fed and its role in sustaining an unsustainable paper money system.

I was intrigued to see that even the Treasury secretary senses that, at some level, the crisis is connected to central banking. As current Treasury secretary Timothy Geithner said to PBS's Charlie Rose: "But I would say there were three types of broad errors of policy, and policy both here and around the world. One was that monetary policy around the world was too loose too long. And that created this just huge boom in asset prices, money chasing risk. People trying to get a higher return. That was just overwhelmingly powerful."

Mr. Rose asked specifically: "It was too easy?"

Mr. Geithner went on: "It was too easy, yes. In some ways less so here in the United States, but it was true globally. Real interest rates were very low for a long period of time."[1]

---

1. "Geithner's Revelation," *Wall Street Journal*, May 12, 2009.

Rarely do we in Washington hear the real cause of the crisis, stated with full knowledge and without the usual hedging. Most don't understand the business cycle and its relationship to Federal Reserve policy. What's more, many of those who do understand how the monetary system operates are not anxious for the general public to find out how it serves the interest of big government, big corporations, and big banks.

Then there are those, familiar with free-market economics, who are well-informed and understand perfectly how the crisis evolved. Since the predictions made by the free-market Austrian economists have been on-target, and the others completely wrong, it is to them we should be looking for the answer to both the cause and solution.

Just as Henry Hazlitt and other Austrian economists knew, in 1944, when the Bretton Woods system was established, that it would not last, many others knew from the beginning that the current system started on April 15, 1971, would also fail. The date may not have been known, but its demise was predictable.

The current crisis, started in 2007 with the break in the housing mortgage market, is now in full swing and signifies the end of the fiat dollar reserve currency system. It is impossible to understand the current crisis without understanding the international monetary system, which has been dominated by our Federal Reserve.

The core of the contemporary problem dates from 2001 when the Fed attempted to forestall recession through low interest rates. Actual interest rates fell well below historical averages and any monetary rule that the Fed claimed to be following.[2] Greenspan slashed the federal funds target from 6.5 percent in January 2001 down to 1 percent by June 2003. He held the rate at this level for a full year before ratcheting them up again to 5.25 percent in June of 2006, a move that popped the bubble he had earlier created.

By way of review, when the Fed lowers interest rates below their natural level on a market, it has the effect of expanding investment beyond a sustainable level. Businesses begin investing as if consumers had the savings to back up the signals that the interest rates are sending. But real resources are not in fact available. There is no new wealth available to make good on investments. The lower interest rates are creating no new capital; they are merely distorting the signals borrowers use to assess risk.[3]

We should also consider the political context of the time. The terrorist attacks on American soil had taken place, and the entire country was moving toward war frenzy. The idea then was that we would not let terrorists beat us economically or politically—fine impulses but also conditions that led to stupid short-term decision making. Part of the drive of the Fed to inflate in the year following the attacks was to create an appearance that we as a nation had not been harmed in any way—that our economy was stronger than ever.

Sadly, Greenspan chose the wrong means to convey this

2. John B. Taylor, "The Financial Crisis and Policy Responses: An Empirical Analysis of What Went Wrong," http://www.stanford.edu/~johntayl/FCPR.pdf.

3. For a long series of articles explaining in detail the role of the Fed, against the few people who claim it had a limited role, see the archive of economist Robert Murphy: http://mises.org/articles.aspx?AuthorId=380.

message. It would have been an ideal time to put the economy on a firm foundation, even to the point of risking recession, rather than providing artificial stimulus that would later prove to be illusory. Everyone in those days was consumed by the drive to not let the terrorists win. Well, the Fed assisted in undermining the foundation of the structure of the American economy and, in the long run, did more damage to American economic prosperity than the attacks of 9/11. Greenspan aimed the gun at the terrorists and shot the economy in the foot instead.

I want to be clear here. The Fed's policy was dreadfully malformed. It was within Greenspan's control to have constructed a better policy. He made terrible mistakes. But this does not mean that the answer would have been better policies alone, tighter controls alone, or better managers of the Fed. We've been through nearly a hundred years of this same repeating pattern, so it is time that we wise up and learn something. When the printing presses are available to the government and the banking cartel, they will use them rather than do the right thing.

The problem isn't with the choices made by central bankers. The problem is that they possess the power to make any choice at all. There is the additional problem that markets are forever having to guess what the Fed is going to do, which creates what historian Robert Higgs calls "regime uncertainty."[4] He goes so far as to use this notion to explain why markets sometimes take so long to recover from monetary

4. Robert Higgs, "Regime Uncertainty: Why the Great Depression Lasted So Long and Why Prosperity Resumed after the War," *Independent Review*, Vol. I, No. 4, Spring 1997: 561–590.

mistakes. Market forces are always working to correct the mistakes made by individuals or government. Since central bank inflation is always disruptive, the market attempts to halt it as quickly as possible. This does not happen on a predictable schedule.

The post-Bretton Woods system has been challenged numerous times over the past thirty years, but the authorities have been able to reprime the monetary pump, distract the masses, and keep it from deflating and correcting the errors inherent in central bank economic planning.

Instability was already apparent in 1987, with a sharp stock market correction called a crash. The Fed reinflated and restored confidence in a broken system. No final payment was extracted for the inflation that has gone on since 1971. Dollar imbalances in the world economy kept being papered over. In 1989, the crash of the Japanese market showed that the international imbalances permitted some of our dollar inflation to be exported to Japan rather than do damage at home. More recently, our excessive purchases have come from China, exporting inflated dollars yet again.

The savings and loan crisis of the 1980s was another effort of the marketplace to rectify the mistakes inherent in the system. Debt, to some degree, was liquidated, but as there were no significant changes in policy the country and the Federal Reserve went back to their old ways, with even more inflation than before.

Japan's market has never adequately recovered from its 1990s slump because it prevented liquidation of bad debt held by the banks. Throughout the 1990s in the United States, the market was arguing for liquidation of debt and elimination of gross malinvestment. But our recessions, the Asian crisis, as well as the Russian crisis were papered over with more inflation. Even the failure of Long-Term Capital Management in 1999 was barely a blip on the economic radar screen.

By the year 2000, the imbalances were more than could be contained. The massive injection of credit for Y2K softened the blow of the 2000 recession, but it was clear by then that the "Big One" was at our doorstep. And I suspect that Greenspan knew it. He energetically contributed to the already very large housing bubble by driving down and holding interest rates very low for several more years. He bought time for himself and the institution he represented.

The collapse of the stock market in 2000, especially the bursting of the NASDAQ bubble, was the beginning of the current crisis, although many want to date the onset in 2007 when the mortgage crisis became obvious. The bull market in stocks had ended long before. The massive inflation that was directed into housing was designed to make people feel better, and consumers once again were enticed to continue their spending spree by borrowing against their home equities, driven up at least nominally by inflationary expectations. Monetary policy was always hostile to savings. Savers were cheated with lower rates of interest. Greenspan's answer to my concerns regarding this point was, more or less, "True, but that's just tough luck."

But prosperity can never be achieved by cheap credit. If that were so, no one would have to work for a living. Inflated prices only deceive one into believing that real wealth has been created. But easy come, easy go. It is fun when the bubbles are forming and many can live beyond their means; it's a different story when they're forced to live beneath their means in order to pay for their extravagance. Like an individual, a whole nation must accept a decrease in the standard of living if the debt-inflationary system finances an illusion of wealth.

Although the Fed was primarily responsible for the financial bubbles, the malinvestment, and the excessive debt, other policies significantly contributed to the distortions that had to be corrected.[5] Artificially low rates of interest orchestrated by the Fed induced investors, savers, borrowers, and consumers to misjudge what was going on. Multiple mistakes were made. The apparent prosperity based on the illusion of such wealth and savings led to misdirected and excessive use of capital. The false information generated by the Federal Reserve policy led to a false confidence that all would be well. This illusion is referred to as moral hazard.

Anything that is seen as protection against risk causes people to act with less caution. Even if their actions may seem risky, someone else suffers the consequences, and moral hazard will encourage bad economic behavior.

Knowing that savings were no longer required to get a loan from a bank, since easy credit came from the Federal Reserve, many a banker and borrower were encouraged to "gamble" on business ventures. It is easy to accept this risk, especially in the boom part of the business cycle, with stock, land, and housing assets all going up in nominal value. Beneath the surface, they were buying into a moral hazard, that is, they were being rewarded in the short term for activity that would in the long

5. For a more detailed account, see Thomas Woods, *Meltdown* (Washington, DC: Regnery, 2009).

term prove to be detrimental to everyone. Competitive pressures in the banking industry made it impossible for most to resist the chance for a quick profit.

Moral hazard, from whatever source, is detrimental because it removes the sense of responsibility for one's own actions. The more socialized the society, the less the sense of personal responsibility for one's own behavior; responsibility becomes collective. Interventionism conditions business people to believe they can enjoy the rewards of the market, yet pass on the penalties to others. That's what's happening today.

Although I'm talking here about moral hazard in the financial sense, the whole notion of the safety net permeates a welfare or socialist state, encouraging carelessness and dependency on the government to deal with any problems that come as a consequence of unwise economic or personal behavior. The only way government can fill this role as protector of last resort is through the sacrifice of personal liberty.

The most serious mistake made by some "progressives," who are allied with us on restraining the Fed, opposing corporatism, militarism, and the social Machiavellians, is that they make an exception for personal economic decisions. They recognize the right to decide for ourselves what our social and religious values are to be, though they do not understand that it is the same as the right to decide how to spend our money, enter into any voluntary economic contract, and reject any economic association we please.

It's bewildering to see some people strongly and correctly wanting to keep the government out of all social, religious, and intellectual decisions, yet also assuming for some reason that the average citizen cannot exist without central economic planning regulating our every move. It's this inconsistency that allows institutions like the Federal Reserve to gain power over money and credit and, unfortunately, the entire economy.

Once it's assumed, as has been the case for decades, that government must protect all citizens against their own actions and compensate for any harm done, the floodgates of preemptive regulations and uncontrolled prior restraint are opened. Although no one proposes that religious or intellectual activities be reviewed by moral engineers in Washington—though some actually try—we are only too happy (or too complacent) to allow the economic planners to review our economic actions, and we expect the government to care for us following any errors we commit or for some unforeseen result of our actions.

Much has been said about the subprime loans encouraged by government regulations made over the decades before the housing bubble burst, but one could argue that all loans that come from credit created out of thin air have an element of being subprime, making them a less than wise use of capital. This is why the euphoria during the boom is excessive, but only on the bust side is it found to be excessive and devastating. The risky loans were pervasive while the financial structure was being built without a foundation. One need not have been a prophet to have anticipated the collapse; logic and understanding made the collapse a certainty.

Those who did not see it coming, and still don't understand why it has occurred, are unaware of how the market works. They are in denial of the shortcomings of the Fed's monetary policy. The world economy cannot be rescued by the same people, or their philosophy, which brought the havoc upon us.

Moral hazard breeds dependency, neglect, and sacrifice of

liberty, tolerance of false monetary doctrines, and promises of wealth without work. Utopian wishes are dreams destined to turn into nightmares. Paper money advocates make promises to the masses in order to appease them, while they are convinced by their own superiority that they can acquire wealth themselves, control the government for the good of the people, and bring paradise to the world.

Artificially low interest rates are achieved by inflating the money supply, and they penalize the thrifty and cheat those who save. They promote consumption and borrowing over savings and investing. Manipulating interest rates is an immoral act. It's economically destructive.

The market rate of interest provides crucial information for the smooth operation of the economy. A central bank setting interest rates is price-fixing and is a form of central economic planning. Price-fixing is a tool of socialism and destroys production. Central bankers, politicians, and bureaucrats can't know what the proper rate should be. They lack the knowledge and are deceived by their own aggrandizement.

Manipulating the money supply and interest rates rejects all the principles of the free market, and so it cannot be said that too free a market caused this mess. The market was not free at all. It was manipulated and distorted. Ironically, free markets and sound money generate low rates, but unlike the artificially low rates orchestrated by the Fed, the information conveyed is beneficial to investors and savers. Only the Federal Reserve can inflate the currency, creating new money and credit out of thin air, in secrecy, without oversight or supervision. Inflation facilitates deficits, needless wars, and excessive welfare spending.

When you think about it, debasing a currency is counterfeiting. It steals value from every dollar earned or saved. It robs the people and makes them poorer. It is the absolute enemy of the workingman. Inflation is the most vicious and regressive of all forms of taxation. It transfers wealth from the middle class to the privileged rich. The economic chaos that results from a policy of central bank inflation inevitably leads to political instability and violence. It's an ancient tool of all authoritarians.

Inflating is never a benefit to freedom-loving people. It destroys prosperity and feeds the fires of war. It is responsible for recessions and depressions. It's deceptive, addictive, and causes delusions of grandeur with regards to wealth and knowledge. Wealth cannot be achieved by creating money by fiat, which instead destroys wealth and rewards the special interests, but more importantly, simply is not real.

Depending on monetary fraud for national prosperity or a reversal of our downward spiral is riskier than depending on the lottery.

Inflation has been used to pay for all wars and empires as far back as ancient Rome. And they all end badly. Inflationism and corporatism engender protectionism and trade wars. They prompt scapegoating: blaming foreigners, illegal immigrants, ethnic minorities, and too often freedom itself for the predictable events and suffering that result.

The Congress, the bureaucrats, and the courts took an unsound monetary system destined to wreak havoc on our economy and made it much worse. Various programs, many started in the 1930s, encouraged and sometimes forced lenders to make subprime loans. The market, though not perfect, minimizes unsound lending practices. Both borrowers and lenders are much more cautious when the risk is borne by the two parties involved rather than protected by the proverbial safety net.

In a structured social welfare–interventionist state, no one becomes solely responsible for his or her own actions. The penalty is diluted and hidden from the victims. Benefits are seen, costs are delayed and difficult to identify. Politicians thrive with arrangements like this, at least until the truth is revealed in the painful period of a correction.

If individuals aren't responsible for their actions as the bubble forms, the responsibility falls on others and to a future generation. Taxpayers, eventually, must foot the bill. High prices, a consequence of inflationary policies, act as a tax on everyone, but hurt the poor and the middle class the most. All bailouts are dependent on the Fed to create new credit out of nothing, the very policy that caused the mess in the first place.

The Community Reinvestment Act of 1977, as well as the Equal Credit Opportunity Act of 1974, contributed in large measure to the excesses in the subprime market by forcing lending agencies to specifically make loans they otherwise would have avoided. The flawed concept of economic equality through force, a socialist notion, prompted legislation like the Community Reinvestment Act, which was really a way of institutionalizing affirmative action in the financial sector, since the borrowers who temporarily benefited (or were exploited) were disproportionately minorities. The very most one might concede is that affirmative action in making loans is based on the good intentions of many who support the programs. But as with all government actions, unintended consequences and new problems result.

The problem is that, in the early stages, government economic planning and affirmative action lending look appealing. More homes are built and more people purchase homes that they otherwise would not have qualified for. Home prices soar and borrowing against the inflated prices is something the government and regulations encourage. The homeowners live beyond their means on borrowed money. None of this would have occurred in a free market with sound money. But the climactic end to this illusion of wealth and home ownership for everyone is logically predicted. The poor are being foreclosed upon. Many will be out on the street. More inflation and government handouts won't solve the problem. The government is broke, and any effort to bail out everyone further prevents the return to sound economic policies. The agony compounds as the system unwinds, just as the euphoria expands on the upswing. Reality has now set in. The con game is over. Proper analysis is crucial, or we stand to lose a lot more.

The poor were deceived into believing government force could get them a home even if they hadn't saved a penny, and it didn't work. But many thrived as the housing bubble developed. Fannie Mae and Freddie Mac executives did well and "escaped" with millions. Even after the collapse many were still able to collect taxpayer-subsidized retirement benefits. Builders made huge profits constructing houses and stashing away profits, enjoying the steady increase in prices. Sale prices frequently exceeded the anticipated price when construction started.

Mortgage brokers, banks, insurance companies, "flippers," landowners, and developers all enjoyed the ride, and many were able to protect themselves. The poor were not so lucky. With the collapse of the imbalances created by the dream of easy wealth, the poor, deceived into believing politicians could deliver the moon, are now unemployed and without a home. The last thing that is likely to save them is a public works program. If the government was completely wrong in allocating massively excessive capital into housing, precipitating the greatest financial bubble in human history, it is hardly capable of making the correct decision as to where capital should be directed in the next decade.

There are many programs similar to the CRA that add fuel to the fire of waste, fraud, debt, and malinvestment. Significantly contributing to the moral hazard, that is, the bad judgment, have been the FDIC, SEC, Fannie Mae and Freddie Mac, HUD rules and regulations, court orders, the IRS, and a credit card mentality of no limits.

GSEs (government sponsored enterprises) such as Fannie Mae and Freddie Mac sent a message to investors and lenders that the Treasury and the Fed would always be there if any problems arose. Foreign investors were definitely more inclined to invest in securitized mortgages knowing that Fannie Mae and Freddie Mac had an open line of credit to the U.S. Treasury. Interest rates were already below market due to Fed policy, but the line of credit lowered rates even more, encouraging more risk taking. Subsidized mortgage insurance produced great incentive for making subprime loans that would have otherwise been rejected. And if there was no Fed, the risk takers all would have thought much more about the consequences of their actions.

Sarbanes-Oxley, a regulatory consequence of the Enron and Long-Term Capital Management failures that imposed massive new costs on American business, did nothing to prevent today's crisis. Our problem today was not caused by lack of business and banking regulations. Many, including Greenspan, now argue that the major flaw in the system was the lack of adequate legislation to control "unbridled capitalism." If only we could have monitored the "derivatives" market, the bust could have been prevented, they argue. Not so! Bureaucratic regulations cannot compensate for government programs and a Federal Reserve policy of inflationism that guarantees gross imbalances in the economy and provides a permanent safety net so that major losses are not felt by the perpetrators.

The only regulations lacking were the ones that should have been placed on the government officials who ran roughshod over the people and the Constitution.

The Fed, short of being abolished, should have been prohibited from creating money and credit out of thin air and exerting monopoly control of the system with authority to set interest rates. These powers, unregulated, have nothing to do with freedom and sound economic policies.

The Treasury should be regulated much more carefully. What it can do with its power is rarely monitored or understood by the Congress. Secret use of multibillion dollars in the Exchange Stabilization Fund that's been available since 1934 is off budget, and the Treasury can spend billions of dollars any way it pleases. It also has "legal" power to be involved in the gold market. Although there's no admission by Treasury, I've always been convinced that the Exchange Stabilization Fund is involved in stock, commodity, and currency transactions by manipulating prices.

As part of the ignored President's Working Group on Financial Markets (Plunge Protection Team), the Treasury, along with the Fed, SEC, and CFTC, will continue to rescue the market any way possible. Unfortunately, it's more likely that its powers will be used to bail out friends at the expense of the rest of us.

Wall Street won't object. It wants protection from downturns and cares little about truly free markets. Wall Street expects and welcomes behind-the-scenes assistance and the more obvious bailouts that are epidemic today. Plans were bold to control the markets for the benefit of the establishment, but evidence is abundant that the markets have shown superior strength to the elites armed with false ideologies.

The post-meltdown bailout economy has been one of the most frightening sights I've seen in all my years in Washington. President Bush, anxious not to be seen as another Hoover (who in fact was a horrible interventionist, contrary to what civics-book history says), embarked on a crazy program. He found himself committed to some $700 billion in bailout money. The Fed has committed trillions of dollars. President Obama followed up with an even larger stimulus package.

This spending will only stimulate sectors of the economy that are failing. This is like trying to rid the world of gravity by throwing things up in the air. It addresses symptoms, not causes. It robs the private sector of wealth that can be used for recovery. The debt buildup crowds out private-sector lending. It perpetuates bad views concerning home ownership. It subsidizes the past while ignoring the future.

The deficit is nearing $2 trillion for 2009. The proposed budget promises to create nearly $10 trillion in new risk. The economist Michael Boskin estimates that all of this will lead to $163,000 in new taxes for the typical American family—that is, if it is not inflated away.[6] Even mainstream economists like Joseph Stiglitz are calling this a robbery of the American people. And the more bailouts there are, the more government gets involved in running companies like General Motors, firing and hiring CEOs. Does anyone really think that the federal government should be in the business of hiring and firing CEOs of companies?

The U.S. debt obligations are unfathomable, approaching $12 trillion. You might say that the entire federal government is one giant toxic asset at the moment. It certainly has no business telling the private sector how to run its affairs. It is in worse financial shape than all the companies in the private sector put together.

And yet someone is getting the money. Mostly it is powerful players in the market, institutions that are regarded as essential to national well-being, such as Goldman Sachs and AIG insurance. In fact, these companies could have been allowed to go bankrupt with no downside for the general population, just like Lehman Brothers was allowed to die. Yes, there would be pain, but at least it would be temporary. The current path is prolonging and extending the pain—while causing a slow death dressed up in fancy clothes.

6. I've appreciated the project of the Competitive Enterprise Institute, BailoutWatch: http://www.openmarket.org/category/bailout/.

CHAPTER 10

WHY END THE FED?

The Federal Reserve should be abolished because it is immoral, unconstitutional, impractical, promotes bad economics, and undermines liberty. Its destructive nature makes it a tool of tyrannical government.

Nothing good can come from the Federal Reserve. It is the biggest taxer of them all. Diluting the value of the dollar by increasing its supply is a vicious, sinister tax on the poor and middle class.

The Federal Reserve's monetary policy has brought us to where we are today—in a tragic economic mess. Though the dollar survives for now, the international financial system built over the past thirty-eight years has been brought down by market forces. The fiat dollar reserve standard that evolved out of the breakdown of Bretton Woods in 1971 has come to an end. That is the significance of the economic crisis in which we find ourselves.

Continuation of the same inflationary policies that led to this disaster cannot revive the current system or bring back the Bretton Woods system of 1944. They are finished. What

it can do is destroy the dollar. Unfortunately, since the housing bubble burst, signaling the end of a monetary era, everything Congress and the Fed have done has set the stage for a dollar crisis. That's very bad news since the rejection of the dollar will create, mainly out of fear and a lack of any other ideas, an even greater crisis than the collapse of the international financial system.

The evidence is abundant that the Fed is at fault and should be abolished. So far, though, all Congress has done is give it even more power as the principal central economic planner.

Karl Marx's Fifth Plank of the Communist Manifesto is clear: "Centralization of credit in the banks of the State, by means of a national bank with state capital and an exclusive monopoly." This does not mean that everyone who advocates a powerful central bank is a communist. It does mean that if one is inclined toward authoritarian rule, a central bank is of the utmost benefit.

A central bank by its very nature is the opposite of a commodity standard of money. A gold standard does not require an authority to run it. If a central bank comes into being when a gold standard is in place, the purpose is to circumvent or eliminate the restrictions the gold standard places on those who want to enlarge the government over the opposition of the people. The only government involvement needed for a gold standard to work is to enforce antifraud laws and contracts.

Inflation and debasement of currencies have been around for a long time. Before modern-day central banks, the government, a king, or a tyrant with monopolistic powers over the monetary system could choose to debase the currency for some ulterior motive, many times to pay for war and expand an empire.

The irony is that once the power over money is used to build the state, in time the very process of monetary debasement frequently destroys the empire with an economic crisis of its own making.

From the time of Constantine I, for six centuries, the Byzantine Empire thrived in international trade and commerce with a gold standard. Not only did Byzantium believe in honest money, it endorsed free trade and rejected the principles of mercantilism. The gold coin, the byzant, was used all over the Mediterranean and known throughout the world.

For 600 years, the byzant maintained its value, keeping price inflation in check while the economy thrived. In 1071, Nicephorous III Botaniates reduced the amount of gold in what was then the world's most used coin. Fighting a war with the Turks was the excuse for the devaluation. Byzantium lost the battle against the Turks, and lost its currency. Financial chaos erupted and brought an end to the Byzantine Empire. Historians claimed the end of Byzantium resulted from "a financial tragedy."

Although the worldwide elites of our day are very powerful and rich and control the central banks, they, too, will face limitations, just as Byzantium did nearly a thousand years ago. The banking elite may be laying plans for even more control through globalization of trade and financial controls in a worldwide central bank managing a new fiat currency, but the laws of economics will prove cumbersome for them to overcome.

The durability of gold as money was verified once again in December 2008. Archaeologists discovered nearly 300 gold coins dating back to A.D. 600. The coins were issued by the Byzantine emperor. The coins were every bit as valuable as they were 1400 years ago, and more.

One must wonder what our Federal Reserve notes will be worth when discovered in some hideaway a hundred, fifty, or even a year from now. There's no way society can build a lasting and prosperous economic system without money of real value that lasts.

To understand exactly why the Fed must go, one must realize that a commodity used as money is needed for a society to be free. It's as much an argument *for* gold as it is *against* a central bank.

We need not dictate the exact commodity to be used as money in a free society, but history up until now has overwhelmingly chosen gold and silver as money.

Gold was naturally selected by people to use in exchange and trade for more than 6,000 years. In 4000 B.C., Egyptians had bars of gold stamped with Pharaoh's name and used them as money. The first real coinage was introduced by the Lydians in approximately 750 B.C.

Certain characteristics made gold a natural choice as money. It didn't become money merely because some government decided to use it as such. A recognizable substance that was easily portable and that had inherent value was called for. Some say money should serve as a store of value, easily divided, scarce, and desirable. Its most important function is to act as a means of exchange to facilitate trade. Most people recognize that prices of all goods fluctuate and the free market adjusts these changes quite efficiently. Some mistakenly think the value of gold is rigid and leads to "stable" prices of goods and services.

Since gold supplies are limited compared to government's ability to print paper money, it indeed does give us much more stable prices. But the value of gold or silver or Federal Reserve notes is affected by their supply and relationship to other commodities. That is why the system of bimetallism, that is, fixing the ratio of gold to silver, was not a satisfactory system in our early history.

Money developed in early history to facilitate trade and avoid the cumbersome transactions required by barter. Today's complex world trade could not exist without money; bartering works only in primitive economies. Sometimes, though, modern economies become primitive and barter returns, such as occurs after wars and in financial crises. If we're not careful, it could happen again to us.

The importance of money is obvious, and though gold may not be rigid in value, it becomes practical because of its scarcity and efficiency in trade.

The monetary unit of account is used as half of every economic transaction, the other half of course being goods and/or services. One could argue that understanding the nature of money is crucial since every transaction depends on the current perception of its value and the anticipated value of the money in the future. Dealing with economic problems is an overwhelming task for a society that is forced to use an indefinable paper currency that may quickly suffer loss of value at the whims of the monetary authorities who have monopoly powers over its supply.

In a modern economy, no matter how sophisticated it may seem or how long in operation, the more an unpredictable fiat currency serves as the reserve currency rather than a nongovernment entity like gold, the more fragile will be the system. Because the authorities can get away with the fraud for decades, the imbalances will continue to grow and will eventually bring the system to a halt. The more definable the unit of account is, the more smoothly and longer the economy will operate. Paper money, politicians, and central banks always fail the test of time.

When the Federal Reserve was established, its purpose, according to the Federal Reserve Act of 1913, was to "furnish an elastic currency to afford means of rediscounting commercial paper, to establish a more effective supervision of banking in the United States and for other purposes." This was pretty broad in scope; look at what it has brought us after ninety-five years: no stability whatsoever and numerous crises of historic proportions.

An *elastic currency!* I've always been fascinated with this term. I think of it more as a method to allow the government and banking authorities to be elastic with their powers to inflate the currencies for whatever goal they seek. They paint it as the Federal Reserve serving as a lender of last resort in order to protect the workers and depositors, but that is not the prime purpose of having an elastic currency.

In an interesting and good sort of way, gold is elastic. It might be said that it is flexible, efficient in dealing with all the factors that affect prices of goods and services and the value of money. It adapts to market forces. Its supply, unregulated, is always adequate. It serves to adjust for settling current account imbalances so much better and smoother than fiat currency does.

Bernanke and Greenspan always conceded to me that the

imbalances in the current account and the foreign deficits we've run up are a serious problem but would never concede that this reflected the shortcomings of the fiat dollar reserve standard. They would never concede that these problems would not have developed with the gold standard.

But gold adapts monetarily and can be "stretched" to serve as money when prices drop as a consequence of high productivity. The purchasing power of gold goes up and is stretched to accommodate more transactions. There's too much concern about an inadequate amount of gold. This is a worry that need not be. Paper may be "elastic" in the sense of inflating and bailing out bad debts, but it also acts like a boomerang as the "stretching" money supply snaps back with both inflationary and deflationary consequences.

Putting money in the right perspective is crucial. Money does not equal wealth; gold alone is not wealth. Some believe that an increase in paper money will provide wealth, yet all it does is dilute the value of the existing money in circulation. Just automatically doubling the amount of gold in circulation may be a lot more fun compared to doubling the amount of paper currency, but it doesn't substitute for productivity and improve commerce and trade. If productivity doesn't go up, even doubling the gold supply will merely push prices up in the gold currency.

Greenspan and I sparred over a definition of savings at one of our hearings. I considered it a bad sign that we were no longer saving and that all we were doing was borrowing and consuming (and that too often the borrowing was possible only because of an increase in home equity as a consequence of inflation). He argued that because the value of most people's homes was going up, this valuation represented "savings." I strongly disagreed and claimed he was confusing debt with true savings. He thought it was perfectly fine for the increased value of peoples' homes to be borrowed against with the funds used for consumer purposes.

If the value of one's home comes from savings and not from artificially inflated prices, there would be no housing bubble. If one puts down 20 to 30 percent on the purchase of a home, the value of the house may fluctuate with the economy for various reasons, but these changes couldn't create a housing bubble that is destined to explode.

Wealth can't come from appreciating the value of a house in the boom phase of a business cycle. If one is a flipper and lucky enough to sell at the right time, he may become wealthier, but there is no increase in national wealth. But even this process does not create new wealth; it merely allows the seller to profit on a quick transaction. Some do manage to benefit from escalating prices, but when the boom ends, more suffer from the consequences of falling prices. Neither process can substitute for true savings. That requires living within one's own means and not consuming one's entire income. Our problems, of course, have been that we, as a nation, have consumed our earnings plus the borrowing required to satisfy our ravenous appetite for consumer goods.

CHAPTER 11

THE PHILOSOPHICAL CASE

The moral argument against the Fed should be simple, and it would be, in a moral society. Once I pointed out that the two weakest arguments for any issue on the House floor are moral and constitutional. And that remains true today. If a society were truly moral, a written constitution would hardly be necessary. The moral principles that would guarantee sound money, and our not needing a central bank to manage it, are honesty, which would reject fraud, and keeping one's word. Contracts should be protected, not undermined by the government.

Looking at the money issue, it's easy to conclude that those who orchestrate and benefit from inflating the currency are no better than the counterfeiters themselves. Yet the process has made it seem that the inflators are serving the public interest by merely managing the currency.

Today we speak of the printing of money by the Federal Reserve. But it's more complex than that. The grand scheme of counterfeiting now occurs with a computer, not a printing press. We allow the Federal Reserve to exert monopoly control over money and credit and interest rates. Law permits this highly secretive, private bank to create credit at will and distribute it as it sees fit.

The chairman of the Federal Reserve can blatantly inject in a public hearing that he has no intention of revealing where the newly created credit goes and who benefits. When asked, he essentially answered, "It's none of your business," saying that it would be "counterproductive" to do so.

The entire operation of the Fed is based on an immoral principle. Congress contributes to the immorality by permitting the process to continue without any true oversight. The immorality associated with money is as much about omission as commission.

Members of Congress, when they knowingly endorse this system of fraud because of the benefits they receive, commit an immoral act. Financing spending in an irresponsible manner, through Fed action or future debt burdens, provides immediate political benefits to politicians.

Congress, though, is a reflection of the people. If the problem was seen as a moral problem and the people were to demand morality in money from their representatives in government, the process would end. But the people endorse the system because they have requested and expect government to provide benefits that can't be provided any other way. Transferring wealth is limited when taxes and borrowing are the only tools the politicians can use. Printing money is required. The cooperation of the people, the politicians, and the counterfeiters at the Fed is based on the immorality of fraud, deceit, and ignorance. As the fourteenth-century French bishop Nicole Oresme said, "I am of the opinion that the main and final cause why the prince pretends to the power of altering the coinage is the profit or gain which he can get from it; it would otherwise be vain to make so many and so great changes. . . . Besides, the amount of the prince's profit is necessarily that of the community's loss."[1]

Depending on the many circumstances, the process lasts for varying lengths of time, but it always comes to an end. As all immoral acts do, it ends with much pain and suffering. The big problem is that many immoral acts, including the inflationary process of a central bank, can satisfy a lot of people for very long periods of time.

When times are good and the benefits are being enjoyed, no one is much interested in breaking up the party or worrying about morality in money. The Fed encourages irresponsible accumulation of personal debt. People live beyond their means with the help of an expansionistic monetary policy. They trade in their futures for the present. They neglect the need to save in order to consume more and more. In this sense, the Fed is the ultimate promoter of consumerism and living for the present. This amounts to a terrible cultural distortion in which short-term thinking wins out over long-term planning.

Yet the party always ends and the license taken to have short-term gratification brings grief and a period of payback. Family life is wrecked and marriages crumble. People are no longer free to move and change jobs. They are enslaved to their high credit card debt, the college loans, their car and home loans. None of these institutions and this type of personal fiduciary bondage

---

1. Jörg Guido Hülsmann, *The Ethics of Money Production* (Auburn, AL: Mises Institute, 2008), p. 104.

was known before the Fed. It simply could not be part of a free society with sound money. We would be living within our means because that's what our money and banking system would reward.

Morality of money is related to morality in politics. Big government breeds corruption. If government has nothing to sell, bribery is useless. But even under today's circumstances, if only men and women of character served as our elected and unelected officials, the bribers would be wasting their time. An easy buck is conveniently rationalized as "just doing business" while they argue that they're serving their constituents' interests by participating in the process.

Trading votes for constituents' benefits is routine. Being a "team player" is necessary to gain a plush committee assignment, and the committee assignment is the vehicle for raising money since one's committee votes are even more valuable than the floor votes that come after the deal has been done. Participation in conferences to resolve the differences between the Senate and House versions is a real attention getter for those who contribute or buy influence in the process.

Donations to campaigns, especially to committee chairs who don't even have campaign races of any note, are the way business is done. It is a quick quid pro quo, a wink and a nod, and it's all legal. Morality is never considered.

In the presidential campaign, Barack Obama raised more than $750 million, breaking all records. This candidate was seen as a man of the people, caring for the poor, the disenfranchised. He is a man who once promised he would limit his spending by accepting public funds. By the end, Wall

Street, the banks, the military-industrial complex, and the medical-industrial complex all got a piece of the action.

Once it was known—very early on—that the media's candidate was picked, the fix was in and the spigots were on. The downward spiral of the economy did nothing to slow the influence buying. As a matter of fact, the records in campaign funding were set *because* the government portion of the GDP is rapidly expanding and is expected to do so for years to come. There's more "stuff" up for auction.

With all the bailouts and nationalization going on, it's more important than ever that one has access to those in power. The process builds on itself. Just as inflationary bubbles expand, political power structures pyramid on themselves as the role of government grows.

To put it simply, the system is morally corrupt. Politicians should nevertheless resist the temptation to participate. Rationalizing that others do it—that's the way the system works—is unacceptable. Sadly, avoiding discovery is the hallmark of a successful politician.

Few understand or decry the immorality of the redistribution of wealth through government force. The fact that many merely desire to help the helpless and create an economically "fair and equitable" society should be irrelevant.

When politicians pass out the benefits or threaten to withhold them unless there is something given in return, it is commonplace for everyone to express outrage once the deed is known. But there's less outrage over the fact that the goodies being passed out were stolen from productive members of society. The transfer of wealth, protected by law, is the much bigger scandal and is rarely addressed.

The great immorality is the system of government that condones transfer of wealth through force. It's only considered immoral if one is caught passing out the loot. It's relatively easy to see the transfer of wealth through the tax system from one group to another. But we have been conditioned that morality is on the side of the redistributionists who grab the moral high ground by arguing that they alone care for the unfortunate and are merely making the system fair. They argue that, without this system, economic suffering would be overwhelming and unfair. Of course, an understanding of how freedom provides for the needs of the greatest number of people totally refutes this notion.

The process of monetary debasement, by inflating the money supply, redistributes wealth unfairly and dangerously from the middle class to the wealthy. It's based on the principles of fraud and is equivalent to counterfeiting. Its goals are achieved through stealth and are difficult for the masses to recognize. Instead, the people are conditioned to believe that easy credit, monetizing debt, and affirmative action loans are reflective of good economic policy and are morally motivated.

The tragedy is only recognized when the fraud of an immoral, unsustainable monetary inflation comes to an end. That is what we're suffering from today.

When arguing for sound money, the great concern I hear from the Keynesians is for the loss of the "benefits" of inflation; the people and the special interests argue that more of the same is needed. The principle of morality in money is no concern of theirs, and they don't want to hear of it. Those who pretend to be sympathetic to markets and small government announce loudly that now is not the time for ideologues who are obsessed with free-market principles, sound money, and balanced budgets to have their way. Now, they claim, is the time for action to rescue the faltering economy.

What they fail to recognize is that they who condemn ideology are themselves prisoners of a deeply flawed ideology.

Pragmatism, urgency, benevolence, fairness, compromise, fear of the future, and the need for safety and security provide the moral cover for an authoritarian approach to rescuing and protecting the people. Those so inclined are not bashful in declaring that sacrificing some liberty to achieve these goals is morally justified and necessary.

The promoters of central economic planning rarely consider that the flawed policies of interventionism were actually the cause of the crisis and won't admit that more of the exact same thing will only dig the hole deeper. Some even see the chaos as an opportunity to expand their long-held belief that authoritarian government is the ideal. Out of fear of the future and lack of understanding how we got into the mess we're in, others postpone their goals of promoting limited government and free markets for a later time.

The seekers of bailouts condemn their opponents as stubborn and selfish ideologues. Of course, when those wanting the taxpayers' bailouts were making profits, they were quite content to support the principle that the profits were theirs and they deserved to keep as much as possible as part of the free-market philosophy.

It's not a question of being an ideologue; it's a question of which ideology one adheres to. It's virtually impossible to be a supporter of no ideology. The ideologue label is used to make the morally principled ideology look confrontational and uncaring. This then makes it seem like the immoral philosophy, based on government force, is morally superior. It's always couched in terms of caring for the underdog and not as a bailout of those who have unfairly been benefiting from an economic system artificially stimulated by an inflated currency that benefited certain industries' CEO salaries and workers' wages and benefits.

Very simply, there can't be a more immoral system of money than one based on a banking monopoly that can counterfeit money in secret with no oversight and protection of the people. The moral argument against the Fed should be enough for decently well-informed people to dispense with it posthaste.

Even the Bible is clear that altering the quality of money is an immoral act. We are instructed to follow the rules of "just weights and measures." "You shall do no injustice in judgment, in measurement of length, weight, or volume. You shall have just balances, just weights, a just ephah, and a just hin" (Leviticus 19:35–36). "Diverse weights are an abomination to the Lord, and a false balance is not good" (Proverbs 20:23). The general principle can be summed up as "You shall not steal" (Exodus 20:15).[2]

The Bible assumed that money was a precious metal and honest weight and measures were to be practiced. The words of Jesus even contain a germ of the Austrian theory of the business cycle, which addresses the problem of unsustainable investments. "For which one of you, when he wants to build a tower, does not first sit down and calculate the cost to see if he

---

2. Gary North, *Honest Money: Biblical Principles of Money and Banking* (Fort Worth, TX: Dominion Press, 1986).

has enough to complete it? Otherwise, when he has laid a foundation and is not able to finish, all who observe it begin to ridicule him" (Luke 14:28–29).

Although some claim love of money itself is the root of all evil, others say that it is dishonesty in money that has been a major source of evil throughout history.

Ayn Rand's defense of honest money meant the outright rejection of paper money. On the issue of "objective standards" for money, she was nearly biblical. Honest money to her was required for a prosperous society. In Francisco's speech in *Atlas Shrugged*, she warned of the day when the paper money system would collapse. Rand stated that if you wanted to know when a "society vanishes . . . watch money." Whenever "destroyers appear among men, they start by destroying money, for money is men's protection and the base of a moral existence. Destroyers seize gold and leave to its owner a counterfeit pile of papers." Paper money to her was a "mortgage on wealth that does not exist."[3]

No great religion advocates governmental fraud in money. All speak of fulfilling one's promises and obligations and respecting other people's persons and property. Central banks, and especially our Federal Reserve, deliberately run roughshod over this principle that has been endorsed for thousands of years by essentially all religious and ethical leaders. Yet the "love" of controlling the money by the powerful is indeed the root of great evil in the world.

---

3. Ayn Rand, "Francisco's Money Speech," *Atlas Shrugged* (Estate of Ayn Rand, 1957), reprinted in *Capitalism Magazine*: http://www.capmag.com/article .asp?ID=1826.

The lack of clarity on morality in politics, economics, and money invites and seduces many who claim to believe in, or once believed in, free markets to accept a partnership arrangement with government.

I recall an early political race for Congress I had in a special election, in 1976, the first I actually had a chance to win. I was truly a neophyte and very naive. But time and circumstances placed me in a position such that the Houston business establishment actually thought I could win. This in itself was remarkable, because there were only three Republicans out of twenty-four in the entire Texas delegation at that time. The congressional seat, the Twenty-second District, had never been held by a Republican. Besides, it was in the immediate post-Watergate atmosphere, which made it even more difficult for Republicans.

Since it was recognized I could possibly win, a meeting was arranged with the Houston business community. At that time, 70 percent of the district was in Harris County, where Houston is located, and a very small percentage was in Brazoria County, where I lived.

One conversation I vividly recall was with George R. Brown, of Brown & Root, which eventually became KBR (Halliburton). He was a Democrat and a known political ally of LBJ's. The two of them modernized politics with fund-raising and by supporting candidates they could control once they were elected to Congress. Brown's support for me was twofold. He opposed the unions that my liberal state senator opponent, Bob Gammage, was identified with. Brown & Root had a large presence in the district. My credibility soared with him because I unexpectedly got into the runoff in the special election.

The reception was cordial and some money was raised—no large amount. My short talk was in the defense of the free market and was as defined then as it is now. In the parting conversation with Mr. Brown, he strongly admonished me, "Remember, for the economic system to work, business and government must be partners." His emphasis was on partnership. I cringed and quickly scooted out the door.

After the election, which I won, my campaign manager urged another fund-raiser with the same city fathers. The announced purpose was to "pay off campaign debt" and to thank them for their support and to recognize their importance. Actually, there was no campaign debt, since even then my rules were firm—never end a campaign with debt. If you lose the election, the debt becomes yours, not the campaign's. Once again Mr. Brown showed up and as we were leaving I heard him ask, "Well, what's my share; what do I owe?" It sounded to me, and probably to him as well, that he had an investment in me and wanted to pay his fair share, like any good "capitalist."

Once I was in office and after my votes and positions became known, the message was clear, and I never heard from him again.

The idea of business and government being partners is nothing new, and even when Mr. Brown said it, it didn't sound sinister. I'm sure he thought it was a rather good system and rationalized that the enrichment of Brown & Root was incidental to the philosophy, not the purpose of the partnership. U.S. government contracts from around the world *just happened*, not because he and LBJ were bosom buddies.

This attitude is pervasive. Over the years, I have heard many businesspeople praise big government, saying how city hall and business must work together. It's a partnership that develops at all levels—city, state, federal, and international (UN, World Bank, IMF, and the multinational development banks). This is all done in the name of capitalism and financed by a corrupt and complacent Federal Reserve money machine. Home builders, highway contractors, bridge builders, and on and on, all support big government projects.

The sad part, when graft, corruption, and financial crisis results, is what gets blamed. Usually it's the free market, and the problems become an excuse to further inflate and enlarge the government while undermining the free market, always serving the special interests. The lack of a moral compass in our entrepreneurial class and the vague understanding of economics have set the stage for the nationalization of the American free enterprise system. It's at our doorstep.

With every passing year, especially since the 1930s, the market economy has shrunk and the government-managed and -subsidized economy has grown. Few care, because our credit has been good and the dollar was perceived as strong; our prosperity lingered as our deficits exploded.

Things have now changed. The loss of the moral principle that defends free markets and sound money has completely eroded the foundation of our economic system. The failure of the economy and the loss of the moral foundation have now set the stage for nationalization. Do the auto executives come to Washington to demand freedom—freedom to contract labor, freedom to retool when they please, freedom to choose the cars they build, freedom from central economic planners regulating their every move, freedom to make profit and keep it, freedom to fail? Do they demand a sound currency that would rectify the international trade imbalances?

No, they come to Washington to demand that innocent Americans bail them out and protect a system that deserves no protection. They never come to demand that the government protect contracts rather than insisting on the government rewriting them. They beg to be taken over, nationalized, partnered with, to obey a car czar and sacrifice every bit of self-respect that they might retain.

There's a lot of blame to go around for bringing us to this point: the Fed, the Congress, the courts, the leeches. But the most abhorrent is the failure of the giants of industry to defend free markets. They are willing to be junior partners with government, believing they have sold out nothing and that better days lie ahead. They believe that they will once again be securely rich and enjoy the fruits of their labor and the benefits of freedom—if they can just get a bailout. Fascism is not on their mind. They rationalize that at times the markets fail and it's legitimate to get a little help from government. They benignly call it a bridge loan to tide them over. But their selfish, narrow greed and distorted concept of the government-business relationship in a free society have set the stage for a sea change in American political structure.

On the House floor, I called it "nationalism without a whimper," and the corporate business community is begging for it. As far as I'm concerned, the nationalization of industry, while retaining private ownership in name only, is just another word for fascism. Gross dishonesty exists today, and if that doesn't include everyone, try *denial* by those who should know better.

Harry Truman, by using an executive order to take over the steel industry during the Korean War, was much more honest with his plans for nationalization. Fortunately, the courts reversed that course of action. Today, there is no principled opposition to the corporate bailouts and the Fed's trillions of dollars of new credit and the takeover of insurance, mortgages, medical care, banks, and the auto industry. The arguments have only been over amounts, financial vehicles, and which political group gets to wield the economic power. If there is no moral argument against the economic takeover of America, there will be no resistance to the dictator who rules over our lives with an iron fist. I already see compulsory national service for all eighteen-year-olds as a program that Americans will be expected to embrace for patriotic reasons.

Over the years, I often wondered how the business leaders of Germany and Italy could have gone along with fascist dictators. Didn't they know how it would end? I'm sure many hoped for the best, and making money in partnership with government was a philosophic position acceptable to both. Totally naive, they believed that they would maintain control over their own destiny.

Once the principle of the use of force by government to run the economy is endorsed, it is conceded that the government can run everyone's life as well. It didn't take long for fascism to evolve from the business partnership that gave us nationalization to uncontrollable militarism. The idea of a *car czar* alarms only a few.

Ever since the first business-government partnership of the nineteenth century, there has been a tendency for these anti-market institutions to spread. The seeds were sown a long time ago, as far back as the planning state of World War I, for fascism to thrive in America. They are quickly maturing into a dangerous political and economic crisis. If we are not vigilant, we will see fascism thrive while liberty is sacrificed.

Justice Louis Brandeis reminded us that crime is contagious, especially when the government commits it. When government breaks the law and defies the Constitution, it sets the standard that makes it much easier for society to do the same. When governments and politicians show contempt for the law, it's a signal that everyone else can do it as well. The real irony is that when the individual lives within the Constitution and tries to hold government officials responsible, they become the lawbreakers. If a situation like this is not rectified, it is destined to lead to violence. The wording on a plaque (which is really a bumper sticker) on my congressional desk reminds every visitor of the moral crisis we face: "Don't Steal, the Government Hates Competition."

CHAPTER 12

THE CONSTITUTIONAL CASE

The Constitutional Convention of 1787 was supposed to be limited in scope. The mandate from the states was to amend the Articles of Confederation. Need for free trade among the states and a sound national currency was high on the agenda. Although there was no admission, by some, the original goal was to discard the Articles of Confederation and write an entirely new constitution.

The Federalists wanted a more centralized and powerful government, complaining that Congress lacked power to regulate domestic affairs, and to collect taxes for national purposes. The anti-Federalists, such as Patrick Henry, worried of the danger of eroding liberty if a centralized government were approved.

Once the delegates were in Philadelphia, plans for changes other than interstate commerce and a national currency quickly emerged. Those who were concerned about the loss of liberty were given the Bill of Rights for additional protection against the encroachment of the federal government on the states.

If the original intent of the Constitution had been followed, we wouldn't be where we are today. The protection against centralized government failed because of too many loopholes in the Constitution—but more so because, over the years, we've had too many people in and out of government demanding that government should guarantee security rather than liberty.

The authors of the Constitution were very much aware of the dangers of inflation and the need for commodity money. Destruction of the continental dollar was vivid in their minds. The journals of the Continental Congress noted that "paper currency . . . is multiplied beyond the rules of good policy. No truth being more evident, than that where the quantity of money . . . exceeds what is useful as a medium of commerce, its comparative value must be proportionately reduced." Further, inflations "tend to the depravity of morals, and decay of public virtue, a precarious supply for the war, debasement of the public faith, injustice to individuals, and the destruction of the honor, safety, and independence of the United States."[1]

The Constitution is clear about no paper money. Only gold and silver were to be legal tender. Since the states caused themselves harm when they issued their own paper money, the states were prohibited as well from issuing paper currency under the Constitution. Article I, Section 10: "No state shall . . . make anything but gold and silver coin a tender in payment of debts." So there you have it, plain and simple: paper money is unconstitutional, period.

The Constitution is silent on the issue of a central bank, but for anyone who cares about its intent, the Tenth Amendment

---

1. Edwin Vieira, Jr., *Pieces of Eight: The Monetary Powers and Disabilities of the United States Constitution* (Old Greenwich, CT, 1983), pp. 12–13.

is quite clear. If a power is not "delegated to the United States by the Constitution," it doesn't exist. There is no mention whatsoever of a central bank being authorized. Even if a central bank were permissible, it could not legally repeal the legal tender mandate for gold and silver coins.

A central bank, theoretically, could exist with a gold standard, but a gold standard doesn't need a central bank to manage it. Without this need, the motivation for having a central bank has to be questioned. It's not difficult to come to the conclusion that the purpose of a central bank, when a gold standard exists, is to get rid of it.

During the convention, the issue of emitting bills of credit (i.e., convertible paper money) was fully debated and defeated. Neither the U.S. government nor the states would be permitted to issue paper money, and only gold and silver would be legal tender. Because of the runaway inflation of the continental dollar in the 1780s and the Founders' disdain for paper, no paper money was officially issued by the U.S. government until the Civil War.

The prohibition of paper money was for convertible certificates. Even this was too great a temptation to be placed in the hands of government. Fiat money was such an outlandish idea that the Founders didn't discuss it. What would they think of our creating trillions of dollars out of thin air and not even bothering to *print* the money? Today it's all done by computers without the slightest hint of oversight by the Congress.

The argument over a central bank started early on; the Federalists supported it and the anti-Federalists opposed it. It was another instance of a Hamilton versus Jefferson argument. Hamilton won the argument early on, and the First Bank of the United States was established in 1791. It was left to expire in 1811, by Jefferson, who was a champion of hard money. The War of 1812, with its high debts and extravagant spending, caused financial problems and deficits bad enough that we again faced the choice between centralization and liquidation. The choice for politicians is an easy one: short-term fix over long-term health. Madison, in 1816, created the Second Bank of the United States. The constitutional argument over this bank in 1819 was of great significance. The seminal decision in favor of central banking, in *McCulloch v. Maryland*, not only was a major setback for sound money; the rationale by the Supreme Court for its decision did irreparable harm to the Constitution.

One side argued, as Jefferson did, that the Constitution gave no specific authority to Congress to establish a central bank. The other side, the majority in the case, amazingly claimed that Congress had all the powers it wanted except for those specifically denied by the Constitution. The whole idea of Article I, Section 8, and the Tenth Amendment was totally ignored. If they are correct in this interpretation, there would have been no purpose whatsoever in putting these provisions in the Constitution.

It was agreed that the "necessary and proper" clause of Article I, Section 8, permitted any law the current Congress thought "necessary and proper." The fact that the "necessary and proper" clause was for exercising enumerated powers—only those powers explicitly granted by the Constitution and, in this case, those found in Article I, Section 8—was ignored.

This gross distortion and undermining of the Constitution by *McCulloch v. Maryland* has done great harm throughout our history and explains how we've ended up with the size of government we have today. It not only opened wide the doors for the Second Bank of the United States, it set the legal stage for the establishment of the Federal Reserve in 1913.

Thus, the Supreme Court established the principle of "implied powers," a completely subjective notion. No longer would there be much chance of paying heed to Jefferson's admonition: "Let no more be heard of confidence in man, but bind him down from mischief by the chains of the Constitution."

In reality, the Constitution itself is incapable of achieving what we would like in limiting government power, no matter how well written. The morality of the people and the character and wisdom of our elected officials are the only things that count. Nevertheless, even with these limitations, we must do our best to "bind them down from mischief" with the rule of law lest the "chains" be used to bind down those of us who oppose the wicked use of government power.

The principle of implied powers, so clearly established in 1819, opened Pandora's box and unleashed the steady erosion of our liberties. This has been especially true in the past century.

We lost twice on *McCulloch v. Maryland* and continue to suffer from both losses. This ruling set the stage for the Federal Reserve Act of 1913 and redefined the idea of "necessary and proper." The Supreme Court has never been a friend of sound money and has rarely been a protector of the Constitution.

The Supreme Court supported making greenbacks legal tender during the Civil War period using the same arguments as Chief Justice John Marshall did in *McCulloch v. Maryland*. The courts have almost always defined legal tender as whatever

Congress wanted—never adhering to the Constitution's clear mandate that only gold and silver coin be used as legal tender and recognizing the prohibition against the "emitting of bills of credit." I am doubtful the courts will ever be helpful to us in restoring constitutional money and ridding ourselves of the Federal Reserve System.

In the case of *Hepburn v. Griswold* in 1869, the Supreme Court ruled wisely and found the legal tender laws unconstitutional. "It has not been maintained in argument, nor indeed would anyone, however slightly conversant with constitutional law, think of maintaining that there is in the Constitution any express grant of legislative power to make any description of credit currency a legal tender in payment of debts," the court ruled. "An act making mere promises to pay dollars a legal tender in payment of debts previously contracted, is not a means appropriate, plainly adapted, really calculated to carry into effect any express power vested in Congress, that such an act is inconsistent with the spirit of the Constitution, and that it is prohibited by the Constitution."

But this ruling would not be allowed to stand, and one year later was reversed by another Supreme Court ruling in *Knox v. Lee* (1870), in which the majority wrote, with evident disregard for the actual Constitution, "It would be sad, indeed, if this great nation were now to be deprived of a power so necessary to enable it to protect its own existence."

But here William Graham Sumner is exactly right: "The legal-tender decision did as great a wrong as the Dred Scott decision, and the latter instance shows us that it is not useless to discuss a constitutional question, even after the court decided it. It will not probably take a war to overthrow the principle of the legal-tender act, but it may take a national bankruptcy."[2]

The Supreme Court was every bit as destructive in dealing with the confiscation of gold in 1933 and in the support it gave for the cancelation of all gold contracts. The government and private issuers of gold bonds were not required to pay in gold. The idea of the government following contracts and enforcing contracts was buried, especially when it comes to money.

The lack of respect for the Constitution even in the nineteenth century set the stage for the Federal Reserve Act of 1913. Fear, misinformation, and ignorance allowed government to ram bad policies down the throats of the American people. This is not unlike giving the president authority to go to war and to bail out those least deserving help in an economic crisis. The rationalization that the state's interest supersedes the interests and the rights of the people is embedded in the arguments as to why the American people had to go along with those who hate commodity money and love central banking.

The Fed was established as a result of the public and banking clamor for an elastic currency, and an elastic currency is nothing more than one that can be arbitrarily increased in volume at the discretion of the monetary managers. Sometimes they argue over who exactly will have the authority to do so, the central bank or Congress or private banks themselves. Increasing the supply of money and credit is the proper definition of inflation, meaning that when the demands were heard for an elastic currency, all they were looking for was a legal

2. William G. Sumner, *A History of American Currency* (New York: Henry Holt and Co., 1874), pp. 58–59.

right to inflate the currency for the benefit of whatever special interests they were concerned for at the moment.

Noble intentions are always used to justify the inflation, but the real reasons are far more sinister. Those who get the control over the money are the beneficiaries, not the people as a whole.

Economist John Maynard Keynes, before he became the champion of inflation, wrote quite correctly of the grave danger of inflation. Like Greenspan, he changed his tune as the years moved on. Keynes stated in his book *The Economic Consequences of the Peace*:[3]

> Lenin is said to have declared that the best way to destroy the capitalist system was to debauch the currency. By a continuing process of inflation, governments can confiscate, secretly and unobserved, an important part of the wealth of their citizens. There is no subtler, no surer means of overturning the existing basis of society than to debauch the currency. The process engages all the hidden forces of economic law on the side of destruction, and does it in a manner which not one man in a million is able to diagnose.

His *Tract on Monetary Reform* from 1923 is also clear:

> A government can live for a long time . . . by print[ing] paper money. That is to say, it can by this means secure

3. John Maynard Keynes, *The Economic Consequences of the Peace* (New York: Harcourt, Brace, 1920), pp. 235–236.

the command over real resources—resources just as real as those obtained by taxation. . . . A government can live by this means when it can live by no other. It is the form of taxation which the public finds hardest to evade and even the weakest government can enforce, when it can enforce nothing else.[4]

Marx's Fifth Plank of the Communist Manifesto mandates a strong central bank monopoly. This was seen as necessary to maintain power over the entire economy and to protect against the encroachment of capitalism.

The Federal Reserve Act of 1913 established the Federal Reserve System to supervise the now fully elastic and easily debauched currency by the unconstitutional powers given to it. Not only would the Fed be able to create money out of thin air, banks were participating and benefiting in the process through fractional reserve banking.

Unfortunately but deliberately, a wall was built between the Federal Reserve and Congress. Congress created the system and could end it. Some say that the great evil is that it's a private bank; therein lies the problem. If that were the only problem, all that would have to be done is to apply the laws against the Fed that apply to all other private corporations. I see the Fed as being much better off than just being private. It's sanctioned by the government, protected by the government, and has the privilege of total secrecy.

The Fed's reports to Congress and hearings are for public

---

4. John Maynard Keynes, *A Tract on Monetary Reform* (London: Macmillan, 1923), Chapter II, Section I.

consumption. Real information is not available to the public or to Congress, the Financial Services Committee, the Domestic Monetary Policy Subcommittee, or to me as a member of all three. I would never be permitted to attend Federal Open Market Committee meetings, where all the big decisions are made; that's totally off-limits.

Their secrecy privilege is protected by law. If the creature can come into being without constitutional authority, it can escape all oversight that other government agencies must submit to. Even the CIA has more responsibility to report to a select few in Congress on its activity, although we can be certain that Congress remains in the dark there as well.

The Government Accounting Office has the responsibility of auditing all government agencies. Title 31, Chapter 7 of the money and finance section of the code describes its duties and powers to audit all financial institutions, including "the Federal Reserve Board, Federal Reserve Banks, Federal Deposit Insurance Corporation, and the Office of Comptroller of the Currency."

That sounds pretty inclusive and clear. But there's a proviso in the law. It goes on to say:

> Audits of the Federal Reserve Board and Federal Reserve Banks may *not* include: Transactions for or with a foreign Central Bank, government of a foreign country, or non-private international financing organization;
>
> Deliberations, decisions, or actions on monetary matters, including discount window operations, reserves of member banks, securities credit, interest on deposits, and open market operations;

Transactions made under the direction of the Federal Open Market Committee; or a part of a discussion or communication among or between members of the Board of Governors and officers and employees of the Federal Reserve System related to clauses (1)–(3) of this subsection.

So when Bernanke quickly refuses to give us information about the trillions of dollars of credit that he recently passed out in the bailout process because that would be "counterproductive," he is really saying, "It's none of your business."

He may well be protected by the law, but he is in defiance of the Constitution. The courts, under today's circumstances, will never rule that the Federal Reserve Board chairman must reveal the information that the Congress or the people seek.

The cries in Washington for more transparency of the whole mess are getting louder every day. The people are sick and tired of seeing hundreds of billions of dollars, i.e., the TARP funds, given to the Secretary of the Treasury without Congress knowing how the money will be spent.

For many decades several members of Congress, among them Louis McFadden, Wright Patman, and Henry Gonzales, have demanded the books at the Fed be opened to inspection by the Congress through an audit by the GAO. Though some concessions have been made, such as the release of minutes three weeks after a FOMC meeting and reporting of some accounting statistics, the core of the Federal Reserve's transactions has remained hidden from congressional scrutiny.

One thing I have noticed in studying the issue is that the more power the Fed has gained, the greater the secrecy they demand. Even today, no reports come from the Fed about providing a rather simple monetary aggregate like the M3 money supply. This is just a matter of counting the amount of money they print (which can be measured in many different ways). The silly reason the Fed gives for this is that they are saving money—saving money by not counting it? Just maybe they think nobody will notice how much money they are creating by refusing to report it.

Today, with the Fed dealing secretly with trillions of dollars worth of loans and guarantees and massively increasing their balance sheet, we are told practically nothing about the deals made with other central banks, which countries and currencies are bailed out, or which "friends" in the business and banking community are treated "more fairly" than the rest.

Transparency is currently a hot issue in Congress because the people have awoken and have sent a message. That's what the spontaneous tea parties organized around the country are all about. This is not a conservative or liberal issue; it's not a Republican or Democratic issue. It is pervasive, across the political spectrum.

I introduced a Federal Reserve audit bill, the Federal Reserve Transparency Act, HR 1207, which Progressive/Socialist (and friend) Senator Bernie Sanders of Vermont introduced in the Senate. I'm convinced that if we had an up-or-down vote on this bill in the House, very few would vote against it. That is a reflection of the concerns the American people hold and how the members of Congress are starting to get the message. Although it may appear that Congress ignores the people, when the people speak loudly and clearly enough, the political animals in Washington respond.

Ever since the establishment of the Federal Reserve in 1913, there have always been at least a few congressmen fighting to expose the Fed for the mischief it causes. Generally, the argument against a Federal Reserve audit has been that certain elements deserve privacy and also that there is no need for the people to know that much about the Federal Reserve. Before 1978, there was no explicit auditing authority for the GAO to examine the books at the Federal Reserve, and that was used as an excuse for no auditing being done. When a request came to Congress and legislation was finally passed in 1978 giving the GAO authority to audit the Fed, the auditing authority was strictly limited and all the important issues were explicitly excluded from the auditing process.

The Fed will deny it, but because it wields so much power by controlling the money supply and interest rates, they have every reason in the world to maintain secrecy in all their activities. This has been known from the time of its inception in 1913, which has always led to demands from at least a few members of Congress for accountability.

Congressman Wright Patman, in 1964, as chairman of the House Banking Committee, had Alfred Hayes, the very powerful president of the Federal Reserve Bank of New York, before his committee. Annoyed with the discussion of transparency, Patman told Hayes: "You can absolutely veto everything the President does. You have the power to veto what the Congress does and the fact is that you have done it. You are going too far."

I actually consider this an understatement, because in the past year or so during this bailout process, the Federal Reserve has garnered an unbelievable amount of power, making it much more influential around the world than the Congress or the President has ever been.

Patman accused the Fed of being too secretive, too independent, and the tool of Wall Street bankers. Though Patman was right in his charges, his solutions did not demand a gold standard. He wanted Congress to assume the powers of money creation and interest rate controls, and his goal was to benefit the poor, small businesspeople, and farmers. Populists then, as they always have and as they do today, want to restore the responsibility for money and credit to Congress. Though a laudable goal, it comes up short of providing a solution to the problems of steady depreciation of the money—only gold can do that.

Nevertheless, Patman, throughout his career (1929–1976), continued to warn of the dangers of excessive Federal Reserve power and persistently demanded an audit of all its activities. Though I went into the Congress for the first time in April 1976, our paths did not cross; during his last year in Congress his health was poor. But I did know and work closely with Henry Gonzales on various issues, in particular the IMF and other banking issues, between 1979 and 1984. He was the chair of the Banking Committee (1989–1995) and led the populist faction for over thirty years (1961–1999), demanding an audit and a curtailing of Fed power. A long time before Patman chaired the Banking Committee, Congressman Louis McFadden of Pennsylvania made the same attempts to alert the American people to the danger of excessive power residing in the hands of the few who control the Federal Reserve and the banking system.

Although the Populists of the past and present have not been hard money advocates, they always shared our conviction that transparency was crucial to any decent reforms. And today, even though many liberal and conservative politicians join the Populists' push for easy money and low interest rates, we all can join together in demanding that the secrecy of the Fed be ended. Reforms will follow, and then we will make the case for constitutional, sound money.

I believe the conditions are more conducive today for achieving some real success in getting an audit than at any time since the establishment of the Federal Reserve System in 1913. When that time comes, I hope for some serious evaluation of the results in light of the Constitution.

CHAPTER 13

THE ECONOMIC CASE

One would think that a moral or constitutional argument against the Fed would suffice, but rarely do Congress and the people respond to such arguments. Drumming up fear concerning economic problems usually is the way the people come around to accepting the panaceas promised by the supporters of central banking and fiat money. A lot of deception, if not outright lies, about economics must be presented to get so many people to go along.

It amazes me how society has advanced technologically since the industrial revolution and through the benefits of great brilliance in physics, chemistry, computers, medicine, electronics, and aerospace. Nations, even with a partial understanding of how free markets work, have benefited tremendously from the abundance created. Yet with all this knowledge, few understand some of the simplest economic truths regarding money. For generations, we have been brainwashed about the necessity of having a central bank to give us a currency that is elastic. We accept a rather bizarre idea with little question. Think about this seriously: if you need money, *stretch* it; that is, just print more of it.

It's as if we still believe that money can be grown on trees, and we don't stop to realize that if it did grow on trees, it would take on the value of leaves in the fall, to be either mulched or bagged and put in a landfill. That is to say, it would be worthless.

Why bright people in an advanced society can conclude that wealth can be increased by merely expanding the money supply is bewildering. I suspect that those who are the real promoters of central banking and fiat money are more motivated by power and greed than they are by sound economic theory. Many others are complacent and trusting and have probably not thought the issue through.

I am convinced that I can get a twelve-year-old to understand the issue of money a lot easier than someone much older. Young people are more open to new ideas; older people are too often fixed in their ways. The total failure of the system we inherited in 1971—confirming the theories of those who believe in sound money and who predicted this outcome—has awakened a whole generation of young people to the issue of money.

They realize that the mess they are inheriting is huge and easily understand how it is related to fiat money and the Federal Reserve. In spite of the tragic consequences of Fed policy for the past several decades, there's reason to believe, out of necessity if nothing else, that sound money will be given a serious hearing in the coming years.

Ludwig von Mises had it right many years ago when he predicted the downfall of all socialist economies, including the Soviet system, for a precise reason. Without a free market pricing system, there's no way to make proper economic decisions regarding supply and demand of products and services. Free-market choices under socialism aren't permitted; the government sets the price and plans production. Government bureaucrats can't know what only markets can determine. Vital in the decision process is the profit-loss mechanism that rewards success and punishes failure. Government ownership of the means of production eliminates the benefits of bad decisions by business managers being punished. Under the socialism and interventionism that we have today, the successful are punished by being forced to bail out the unsuccessful.

We don't have socialism of our markets yet. When we do place wage and price controls on our economy, the market economy teeters or collapses, but generally in the past they have been removed and the economy recovers. Where we do have socialism is in money and credit and setting interest rates. This has been especially true since 1971 when the Bretton Woods Agreement ended and the dollar was delinked from gold.

By manipulating the supply of money and setting interest rates, the Fed has practiced backdoor economic planning. The Fed essentially keeps interest rates lower than they otherwise would be. In a free market, low rates would indicate adequate savings and signal the businessperson that it's an opportune time to invest in capital projects. But the system the Fed operates discourages savings, and the credit created out of thin air serves as the signal for investors to spend, invest, and borrow excessively, compared to a system where interest rates are set by the market.

This causes a major problem. A boom results, and overinvestment and excesses are built into the system, creating a bubble. A recession or depression doesn't come for some extraneous reason; it is a predictable result of the excessive credit and artificially low interest rates orchestrated by the Federal Reserve.

The longer the good times last, the greater the correction will be. Our current boom, except for a few minor interruptions, has been going on since 1971. It's my opinion that it stopped in 2000. The Fed was able to create the housing bubble subsequently, but that has turned out to be the last hurrah. Today, we're witnessing the consequences of this very foolish policy.

Most economists and politicians insist on defining inflation as a rising price level. Rising prices are a consequence of monetary inflation and are harmful. Mises claimed that this confusion over defining inflation was deliberate and mischievous. If it's only a price problem, then blame can be placed on profiteers, speculators, labor unions, oil companies, and price gougers. This deflects attention from the real source of the problem, the Federal Reserve and its money machine. It's because so many are convinced that consumer and producer price increases are caused by these extraneous reasons that wage and price controls are resorted to, while the Fed's role in the inflation is ignored.

The silliness of this understanding is that once prices rise at an unwelcome rate, the blame is placed on a robust economy. In a free market, a robust economy causes prices to go down. A healthy cell phone or computer market, even in an age of inflation, will lower prices. Yet the Fed's solution will be to purposely slow down the economy and decrease demand to lower prices, which works with a lot of pain. This attitude reflects the shortcomings of a fiat monetary system managed by the Fed.

The Federal Reserve is responsible for the boom-bust cycles. It's responsible for price inflation, recession, depression, and excessive debt. Although the central bank can get away with mismanagement of the economy for long periods of time, its policies are always destructive. Unchecked, the policies of a central bank lead to financial chaos, an example of which we are now experiencing.

The fact that the Fed accommodates politicians is a good reason few challenge the Fed's authority. Spending gets members of Congress reelected by providing the goodies that constituents have become dependent on. There are limits on how much taxation the people will tolerate and how much the government can borrow without forcing up interest rates. The convenience of the Federal Reserve monetizing the debt satisfies a lot of people—until the day comes that we suffer the consequences with an economic downturn and higher prices.

Higher prices represent a depreciation of the value of the dollar and are a tax on the people. The tax is borne by the middle class and the poor. The early users of the money are the beneficiaries; the government, the banks, and the large corporations.

This is a deceitful, unfair, and corrupt system. Not only does it transfer wealth from the middle class to the rich, it can postpone payments to the next generation just as borrowing does. The bills incurred in the past two to three decades are now coming due. The inordinate amount of debt must now be paid off or liquidated. Loss of the value of stocks or homes is easily understood, but the *value* placed on these assets represented a gross dislocation of the system as a result of the Federal Reserve's policy.

Excessive debt of a country or a people, once it reaches a certain point, is unpayable and must be liquidated. That point is almost impossible to accurately predict, since it will vary from one situation or country to another. One thing certain is that we as a country, and probably the world, have reached that point.

Individuals and corporations can default and debt is liquidated. When the need arises, liquidation is necessary and beneficial. The market today is demanding this liquidation; the politicians and the Fed are doing everything conceivable to prevent it, but they are only prolonging the agony.

Governments don't default in the conventional manner. They default by debasing the currency, reducing the value thereof, through inflation. If the money loses 50 percent of its value, the real debt the government owes is reduced by the same percentage. This is the plan: massive debt and inflation to bail out friends, pretending to prop up the economy and liquidate debt. It never goes as planned. John Maynard Keynes knew that in a correction it is necessary to lower wages. That's why he supported inflation to force real wages down and do it without confronting labor with the need to lower nominal wages.[1]

Unintended economic consequences that even the central planners did not anticipate result. The worst is economic chaos

1. For a thoroughgoing refutation of Keynes, see Henry Hazlitt, *The Failure of the "New Economics"* (Auburn, AL: Mises Institute, 2008, 1959).

leading to political chaos that threatens not only the poor and the middle class but the wealthy establishment as well. Wealthy corporate owners in fascist Italy and Germany did not survive the tragic outcome of the 1930s and 1940s.

The economic ramifications of the Fed's inflationary policies are endless. Due to easy credit, housing prices soared above reasonable levels. Borrowing against these increased values to increase consumption was exactly what the monetary authorities encouraged. Naturally, a bubble formed and had to eventually deflate. Now the Fed, Treasury, and Congress spend trillions of dollars trying to stimulate housing and get the price of houses higher once again. This they do even though market forces are demanding fewer houses due to overbuilding.

The central planners have become price fixers. It's not a whole lot different than imposing wage and price controls at various times to correct rising price inflation. One attempt is to keep prices from dropping; the other is to keep prices from rising. In doing either, they are eliminating the most important mechanism needed to adjust supply and demand and rejuvenate markets. This represents a grave danger. When interventionists interfere too much with free-market pricing, we move toward a socialist system that in the twentieth century was proven to be unworkable.

The Bernie Madoff fraud case received plenty of attention, and rightly so. Adequate antifraud laws are on the books, and fraud is something every state is capable of handling. The fraud involved in the Enron scandal was prosecuted under Texas state law. Yet the consensus was that there weren't enough SEC regulations controlling these sorts of things, even though it was active traders, not regulators, who first discovered the problem. Congress accommodated and quickly passed the Sarbanes-Oxley legislation. Just as the SEC regulations of the 1930s aggravated and helped to prolong the Depression, the bear market starting in the year 2000 has been aggravated and prolonged by Sarbanes-Oxley.

The argument following the Madoff revelation of a $50 billion Ponzi scheme prompted outcries about the deficiencies of the SEC and that we needed even more SEC regulators on the job. We have 3,500 bureaucrats in the SEC, and the argument is that we don't have enough. Of course that's enough, although the truth is that 20,000 SEC regulators wouldn't suffice because they can't police every business transaction and prevent fraud from being committed. We don't expect a policeman in front of every house in the country to prevent our homes from being broken into.

The idea that the SEC and more Sarbanes-Oxley legislation will protect us against evildoers in the marketplace will not help us. The idea that we can depend on the SEC to protect us significantly contributes to *moral hazard*. More risks are taken believing the government will protect us, and our guard against evil is diminished.

Easy credit by the Fed sets the stage for excesses, both honest and dishonest. Government insurance, like the FDIC and mortgage insurance, reassures us and the banks that everything will be safe and that we'll be protected. The current programs of endless bailouts for everyone provide plenty of incentives to take risks that most would not otherwise have taken.

The government may be able to guarantee our bank accounts up to $250,000, but what it can't protect against is the devastation caused by collapsing financial bubbles and a depreciating currency. Deflating financial bubbles and inflating the cost of living are problems that only scoundrels at the Fed can deliver to us. All the regulations in the world on the economy won't help. Regulations must someday be directed toward the more deserving targets, such as the Fed, Treasury, FDIC, SEC, and the Exchange Stabilization Fund.

The entire system of fiat money and fractional-reserve banking is like a super Ponzi scheme (if we can't pay it back, let's just create more!) and is the source of our problems. Why should we be surprised that, if our government runs a Ponzi scheme, some people feel morally justified doing the same? When did we accept this idea that governments have license to do what they want without moral restraints, and the people must live by a different standard? The answer, of course, is that government must follow the same rules that moral people are expected to.

One of the great dangers that exists once the problem breaks out from collapsing financial bubbles is the cry for protectionism. The Smoot-Hawley Tariff Act of 1930 is the well-known protective tariff that compounded and prolonged the Great Depression.

Today there's general agreement that protective tariffs are bad, and no one runs on a platform pushing tariffs as Hoover did in 1928. That doesn't mean there's not agitation for protection, whether it's for steel, cars, textiles, or agriculture, but hopefully a significant tariff is not in the works.

The issue is that problems of trade imbalances are also a consequence of Federal Reserve policy. Our trade deficits, a very serious problem, have been compounded by our privilege of issuing the reserve currency of the world. This gives us license to inflate and export dollars as if they were gold. This, plus excessive taxes, excessive regulations, and overpriced labor, causes our jobs to be exported.

We can't solve our trade problems with tariffs. They make things worse. We can't solve the imbalances without addressing the subject of money and the power the Federal Reserve has over the economy.

The simplest way to understand the idea of tariffs is that, in a free country, the people have the right to spend their money any way they want. If it's to the advantage of poor people to buy tennis shoes from China, they should have the right to do so.

Tariffs are legal under the Constitution. If we had a constitutional-size government and no welfare-warfare spending, a uniform tariff to cover the cost would certainly be a better way to raise revenue than an income or value-added tax.

Tariffs that protect excessive executive salaries, excessive wages, businesses that suffer from excessive taxation and regulations, or bad business decisions only prop up inefficiencies. The problems contributing to the inefficiencies must be removed. We shouldn't add another problem and another tax to the mess. Tariffs are taxes.

Today, though, tariffs are less likely to be imposed; competitive devaluations to gain an edge for exporters are common. Sound money and no central bank would prevent such a problem and diminish the need for protectionism.

There are many economic ramifications of a central bank like the Federal Reserve operating a totally fiat monetary system. The power to practice central economic planning is too much for the money managers to resist, and the swollen ego of a Fed chairman only encourages mischief.

The ease of financing spending by the Congress with the help of the Federal Reserve makes huge deficits a foregone conclusion. It's *cheaper* in the short run to inflate than it is to borrow and much more palatable than immediate taxation to pay the bills. If a country could not borrow or inflate its currency, its government would be much smaller and the country more prosperous and safer. Needless wars would not and could not be fought.

In the long run, the seductive way to finance government's extravagant spending ends badly. It's never cheaper, and the real costs are significantly higher. Early on, it appears that it's a neat trick to pay the bills this way, and politically it's more acceptable. But the cost to everyone concerned for the economic havoc that results from the inflationary bubbles and the corrections required are far more than anyone bargained for. Instead of a free lunch, the real costs are much higher than anybody anticipated when all the misery of a depression is tabulated.

Everybody recognizes difficult economic times when the predictable recession or depression hits. The problem, though, is that with the brainwashing in economics most Americans have received, the people are unaware of the cause of the problem and the policies needed to restore the economy. Too often the people, the politicians, and the central bankers demand more of the same—more spending, more deficits, more regulations, and above all else, more inflating of the currency—none of which will be helpful. Instead, they compound the problems.

People worry what would happen in a world without the Federal Reserve. My answer is that you would enjoy all the privileges of modern economic life without the downside of business cycles, bubbles, inflation, unsustainable trade imbalances, and the explosive growth of government that the Fed has fostered. You would also disempower the secretive cartel of powerful money managers who exercise disproportionate influence over the conduct of public policy. Without the Fed, Keynesian-style macroeconomic planning that has done so much harm would be no more. (I discuss this at greater length in the final chapter.)

Such are the benefits. But people still worry how banking might work. It would work like any other private enterprise system. Walmart might enter the market, as it wanted to but was prohibited from doing. It would be a truly competitive system that any entrepreneur would enter. But would this be "wildcat banking" of the sort that is frequently condemned from the nineteenth century? No more so than we have "wildcat restaurants" or "wildcat shoe companies." Markets are self-regulating, responding to the wishes of consumers. It would be the same in banking.

In any case, most of the tales of nineteenth-century banking are mythical. The problems of that century's monetary and banking system were imposed by government. There were periodic suspensions of payment, inflationary wars, crazy price-fixing rules under the bimetallism system, and other forms of debt finance. These were problems with government, not the free market. The free-market system worked rather well. In research published by the Minneapolis Fed, two scholars have looked closely at the banking system from 1830 to 1860 and found that it was remarkably stable and safe, with no widespread fraud. Bank failures were fewer than people believe, and importantly, there was no "contagion" effect, that is, a failure of one bank didn't spread to other banks.[2]

This is not entirely unexpected. The bad reputation of nineteenth-century American banking—which existed during what was then the most explosive increase in prosperity ever seen in any country in the history of the world—is largely the result of turn-of-the-century propaganda agitating for the creation of the Fed. We need to look at the facts. And the facts do not surprise us, once we consider that money and banking in a free market would operate like any other normal business enterprise, subject to profit and loss tests and punished or rewarded in the market based on consumer behavior.

We no more need to worry about banking in a post-Fed era than we worry about groceries, shoes, or software now. They are provided by the market and not some distant central-planning apparatus that possesses neither the knowledge nor the incentive to do it well.

To save ourselves from economic and political disaster, a dramatic change in the conventional wisdom of economic policy by our leaders is vital. Fortunately, our numbers are growing and more people than ever, especially young people, are now aware of the menace we face from the Federal Reserve and understand the importance of sound money.

---

2. The proof of these assertions can be found in remarkable detail in Larry J. Sechrest, *Free Banking: Theory, History, and a Laissez-Faire Model* (Auburn, AL: Mises Institute, 2008, 1993), pp. 95–142.

CHAPTER 14

THE LIBERTARIAN CASE

So I believe that there is no more economic or constitutional justification for the existence of the Federal Reserve. When honesty prevails, there are only economic arguments *against* the Federal Reserve. There are no benefits except to some undeserving special interests. There is an ultimate downside to ignoring all the arguments against its existence, one that cannot be tolerated by anyone who is concerned about protecting liberty, and that is the expansive growth of government that inevitably results. There's always a trade-off. When government grows, liberty suffers. This happens no matter what justification is given for the government programs being financed.

Those who (possibly unconsciously) seek socialism, fascism, interventionism, or corporatism always support central banking. Some sincerely seek a central bank as a tool in economic planning to make up for the perceived shortcomings of the free market. Although many who support a central bank will claim that growth of government is not their goal, the result is otherwise. It's the nature of the beast.

Remember that the people who run the Fed are just regular people, as flawed as anyone else. The only difference is that they have massive power to break civilization. Any institution that can do this is by nature tyrannical and is specifically what the Constitution was trying to prevent. Authority to create money gives credibility to legalized counterfeiting. Some supporters of this power believe that the money managers should and will be restrained in creating money for any reason other than for humanitarian purposes. This expectation of self-restraint never works out in the end.

As we have seen time and time again, central bankers have big egos and quickly adapt to the potential power they wield. Then there is also the political pressure to accommodate the deficits that politicians thrive on. Talk about moral hazard. This corrupt method of paying the bills and avoiding direct taxation only serves to institutionalize a system that breeds contempt for liberty and self-reliance, while feeding the growth of big government.

In the early years of an inflationary bubble, the benefits of central banking exceed the costs. When the bills come due, it's hard to identify the victims. Those who do suffer from the inflation and lost jobs rarely see the connection between the Federal Reserve monetary policy and the suffering that comes as a consequence of financing big government in this evil manner.

The monetary system is used to finance welfare for rich and poor, and for fighting unpopular wars. If the people knew the real costs of the welfare-warfare state, they would rebel. But during the boom phase of the business cycle, there seem to be no real costs due to the artificial increase of value of houses and stocks. Then the bubble bursts and the truth becomes known: the prosperity was based on a fiction.

But by then, the government has taken over the economy and our lives and made foreign commitments that can't be met. There is extravagance in both domestic and international commitments. We can no longer pay the bills for social welfare or maintain the empire overseas. How many times do we have to see this happen before we change the fundamentals?

In the process, liberty is compromised every time a new welfare program is established or a new war is entered into. When danger breaks out as a consequence of our policies, inevitably the authoritarians, already in charge, use the problems they created to tighten their grip over the people and the economy.

Terrorism is a serious problem, but if it's not seen as blowback from our unwise foreign interventions, then the only solution offered will be more government control of our lives. We don't change foreign policy; we merely regulate the innocent American people by abandoning the Fourth Amendment protection of their privacy. Those who wanted bigger government anyway conveniently used the problems—such as the 9/11 terrorist attacks—to build fear in the people so they practically beg the government to protect them from harm.

It's quite similar in economic affairs. Excessive spending and the Federal Reserve money machine bring on all kinds of economic problems in the corrective phase of the business cycle they create. The cry once again is for government, the perpetrators of the crisis, to come to the rescue with even more government, which requires more sacrifice of liberty.

The cycle is continuous. At first personal liberty is nibbled away at, but the appearance of prosperity continues. Later on, the worse the crisis, the greater is the threat of tyrannical government entirely taking over our lives and the economy.

This attitude can best be understood by what President Bush said on CNN on December 16, 2008, when he proudly announced: "I have abandoned free-market principles to save the free-market system." Astounding and preposterous!

Unfortunately, most Americans agree with him. They agreed after 9/11 that abandoning privacy protection by the Constitution was required to keep us safe and alive. "How else," they asked, "can you enjoy your freedom?" How could they not see the contradiction in that? The President's statement is quite similar to the excuse for burning a village and killing civilians while being unconcerned, during the Vietnam War, about collateral damage. "Destroying the village," they claimed, "was required to save it."

The principle here is that we are expected to accept without question that we should welcome government action that destroys liberty to save it. It is precisely this idea that urges us to accept the destruction of the dollar in order to save it.

The whole process would be virtually impossible without the seductiveness of a paper money system managed by a monopoly authority. Brute force at times is used by tyrants to come to power, but they quickly gain control over the monetary system to keep themselves in power.

When a society is relatively free, such as ours, it is through the use of deficits, taxes, fear, and fiat money that power is solidified. The authoritarians need the central bank for this takeover.

Those who have, on principle, correctly argued against the

tax-collecting tactics of our government and the unconstitu-
tionality of our monetary system find that their punishments
can be even harsher than that of rapists and murderers. As the
iron fist grows in size and the invisible hand influence on the
market is diminished, we will see a transformation of America
that spells the end of a grand experiment in human liberty.

All the actions of Congress, the administration, and the
Federal Reserve to run the economy are designed to promote
the public good, and the results are a disaster. None of the ongoing bailout programs could exist without the Federal Reserve.
This process represents an iron fist. A hands-off attitude represents a more sensible approach—allowing the invisible hand of
free markets to function and correct the imbalances.

It has been said that no war has been fought without inflation. If we could ever devise a monetary system where inflation was absolutely prohibited, the chance of war breaking out
would be greatly reduced. If we had to immediately pay for
our foreign entanglements, people would not tolerate paying
the bill with higher taxation. It's the meddling in the internal
affairs of other nations that brings about the conditions that
result in armed conflict. Not initially financing foreign intervention would make us much less likely to get involved in
no-win, totally unnecessary wars.

Our carelessness in allowing our government, with congressional complicity, to finance foreign entanglements with Federal Reserve credit makes it easy for Congress to neglect its
responsibility to avoid any war that is not specifically declared
by Congress. Whether it's fighting illegal wars or financing
them with fiat money, lack of respect for the Constitution and

congressional apathy for its responsibility got us into the crises in which we find ourselves.

There's strong support for the current system, especially when the boom part of the cycle is still in place. The beneficiaries are numerous and well represented in Washington.

Military spending is said to be needed to make us safe. The result is that the military-industrial complex thrives—and we're made far less safe and much poorer.

Spending on housing programs and Federal Reserve–driven low interest rates are designed to get more people into homes of their own. The result is that government bureaucrats and politicians benefit. Builders, bankers, mortgage companies, insurers, and developers thrive, and when the bubble bursts, the poor for whom the programs were designed lose their homes and their jobs.

This is true in every government-subsidized program, including medicine, banking, education, and agriculture. Fiat money looks like a panacea. The results are tragic: poverty and chaos ultimately ensue, and powerful special interests demand a bailout from the victims.

If we're not careful, a lot of anger will result from the collapse of this house of cards that the bank of paper built.

The American housing market was built on a financial structure with smoke and mirrors. It's dangerous because today's wealth is shrinking and the same people who benefited during the boom years are still in charge, and their sole goal is to maintain wealth and power and come out on top. The special interests benefited and will need to find victims to pay the bills. All the efforts we hear about in Washington are designed to position the winners in such a way that they can pick up the pieces and pass on the bill to the innocent. This process will not go smoothly, and those who suffer will soon realize that some Americans are more equal than others.

The worse the economy gets, the more power Congress is willing to grant to the Federal Reserve. Who would have ever believed that it would come to this? Trillions of dollars created and distributed by the Fed with no requirement to submit to any oversight.

Nationalization goes on with hardly a whimper from Congress or the people. The buying up of corporate assets is financed through the inflationary policies of the Fed, which is the very process that brought our economy to its knees.

As a way to patch up the system, there is now new talk of the old Keynesian dream of a world currency. I seriously doubt that it will happen. It will falter for the same reason that it has always faltered: nationalist pressure. It is one thing to create a new composite currency for Europe. Not even that is entirely stable. But the world elites will not likely get their act together in a way that would do the same for the world.

I'm happy about that. It is true that a world currency would achieve great gains in terms of efficiency. The classical gold standard was a world currency of sorts, albeit with different names for national currencies. This is an ideal I would like to see restored. But a world currency of fiat paper money would be even more vulnerable to inflationary pressure than the current system. The last check on inflationary finance that remains in the system is the prospect of a falling value of one currency relative to others. A new world currency would remove that one check, however ineffective it is.

There are other outcomes of the current crisis that are more likely, and even scarier. The great threat that we will likely face will be the willingness of our policy makers to bring an end to the "depression" as they claim was done in 1941: with war. We're hearing this ridiculous argument all the time, that the Depression only ended with World War II, as if killing millions of people and giving up all consumer goods are good for the economy. We have a dangerous foreign policy; we follow foolish economic theories; and the people, it's argued, need a distraction. Too often that distraction is war.

There is a much better alternative.

CHAPTER 15

THE WAY OUT

I'll tell you what I think about the way
This city treats her soundest men today:
By a coincidence more sad than funny,
It's very like the way we treat our money.

The noble silver drachma that of old we were
So proud of, and the recent gold coins that
Rang true, clean-stamped and worth their weight
Throughout the world, have ceased to circulate.

Instead, the purses of Athenian shoppers
Are full of shoddy silver-plated coppers
Just so, when men are needed by the nation,
The best have been withdrawn from circulation.

From *The Frogs* by Aristophanes, about 400 B.C.

Even in 400 B.C., as Aristophanes explains, and in ancient Egypt as described in the Old Testament, dishonesty in maintaining sound money coincided with the absence of moral leaders and excesses in foreign military aggression. Our money has gone bad. Our financial system is a mess. Abuse of power and abuse of money bring a nation down.

More people are coming to understand that the Federal Reserve is responsible for the crisis we're in and that it must be ended. Total U.S. debt is at a historic high. It is now greater than 350 percent of GDP. The worst this debt was previously was 300 percent in 1933, not a very good year for America. In 1971, the year Bretton Woods ended, this debt was a more sensible 150 percent of GDP. Since 1971, with the new fiat dollar standard established, the debt grew exponentially as one would have expected with no restraint on the Fed to create new money out of thin air. With growth now decreasing rapidly and U.S. government debt expanding by trillions of dollars each year, this number will quickly soar.

Today we would be hard-pressed to find any movement in the right direction by our leaders. Just in the past year, we have had a barrage of new programs, all based on bigger government, more dollar debasement, and greater power given to the Fed and the executive branch of government. These new federal programs include the Primary Dealer Credit Facility, the Term Auction Facility, the Term Securities Lending Facility, and the Asset-Backed Commercial Paper Money Market Mutual Fund Liquidity Facility. These are in addition to the routine technique of low interest rates and low reserve requirements directed by the Federal Reserve to keep the new money flowing.

It's sad, because our future hangs in the balance, and what we do is crucial to the outcome.

Congress passed the first stimulus package of more than $100 billion in 2008. The Troubled Asset Relief Program (TARP) of $700 billion became law in October 2008. The new administration promised to pass another stimulus package early in 2009, worth up to a trillion dollars. It is engaging in every manner of tricky finance that will end in effectively nationalizing the banking system.

Despite the fact that there are no beneficial results, the worse the economy gets, the greater are the demands for more of the same. The total commitment at the end of 2009 will exceed $9 trillion.

There is another path, but it requires a complete turnaround. It requires only the political will to unplug the machinery of the Fed. Contrary to what people might think at first, this will not mean an end to the financial system as we know it. In a post-Fed world, we will still have the dollar, banks, ATMs, online trading, Web-based systems of fund transfer—none of this is going anywhere. What will be added to the system will be vastly more financial options that are currently being kept at bay, including trading and contracting in many different currencies and new, sounder investment opportunities.

When we unplug the Fed, the dollar will stop its long depreciating trend, international currency values will stop fluctuating wildly, banking will no longer be a dice game, and financial power will cease to gravitate toward a small circle of government-connected insiders. The entire banking industry would undoubtedly go through an upheaval of sorts as sound banks thrive and unsound banks go the way of the investment banking industry of last year: out of business as they should be. Those who are dependent on Fed welfare would have to clean up their act or shut down. Depositors would become intensely aware of which banks are sound and which are not.

Returning again to the theme at the outset of this book, the only unique power that the Fed possesses is the power to inspire and support the creation of new money out of nothing. Who needs that? Banks like it. Government likes it. High-flying financiers like it. But the people do not benefit—just the reverse. A lesson that was taught by the classical economists that remains true: there is no ideal supply of money in a society. Any quantity of money will do, so long as the quality of the money is sound. Prices adjust based on the existing money supply. New quantities of money injected into society confer no social benefit. If production rises and the money supply remains stable, the purchasing power of the money will rise. If production falls while the supply of money remains stable, the purchasing power of money will fall.

We should think of money as nothing more than it was at its origin: a market-created good that emerged out of trade. The most valuable commodity in society, the one good that could be traded for all other goods and thereby help facilitate complex exchange, emerges as money, whether that be beads or animal skins or jewels or precious metals. Gold became money because it had all the properties people look for in a good money. Government had nothing to do with it.

In an ideal world, the Fed would be abolished forthwith and the money stock frozen in place. That doesn't mean that there would be no more credit; rather, credit would be rooted in money saved, not money created. Congress would remove the Fed's charter, and the president would stop appointing Fed governors. Its buildings could be used for other purposes, perhaps bought by private banks that would operate as regular businesses. At the same time, the dollar would be reformed so that it again would become redeemable in gold. The federal government's gold stock could be used to guarantee this convertibility at home and abroad. All remaining powers associated with money could then be transferred to the U.S. Treasury, but now there would be a check on what government did with its power.

The gold standard with no Fed would impose discipline. A new culture would emerge quickly in Washington. There would be a new clarity about the cost of wars and government programs. Just as in our household budgets in hard times, lawmakers would realize that they can't do all things. They must make choices. They must make cuts. Accounting rules would come to rein in ambitions, just as in the rest of the real world. We might even see the emergence of a new generation of political leaders who speak frankly and do what they say.

While a gold standard would be a wonderful change, we shouldn't wait for one before we end the Fed. The dollar has a preeminent role in the world economy. It benefits from its long history as a hard money. This will not change in a post-Fed world. The dollar could continue on as it is today, and its value would start to rise once markets were convinced that the money supply would be fixed.

The federal government would finance its operations the way that state governments do today. Note that states do not have miniature central banks and they manage just fine. The money that the state governments spend is taken in by either floating bonds or by taxation. The legislators and executives are on a short leash in every way. They raise or cut spending based on real factors. Also, the bonds issued by states and municipalities are evaluated and priced by the market. They contain a default premium based on their soundness.

In the same way, without a Fed, the pricing of the debt of the federal government would become more realistic. There would be a built-in default premium that is absent from the current system, which deludes people into believing there is such a thing as a 100 percent safe way to earn interest on money. I have no doubt that ending the Fed would lead to the introduction of a substantial discount on government-issued bonds relative to how they trade now. But this is a very good thing, a truth-telling moment. The value of the debt will fluctuate based on the market's assessment of government policy. Some new, expensive war or corporate welfare program, and the value would fall, as it should, meaning we would have fewer of both.

An end to the money-creating power and a transfer of remaining oversight authority from the Fed to the Treasury would be marvelous steps in the right direction. But let us stretch these ideas a bit further and reconsider the entire idea of a government monopoly on money. The Founding Fathers never set out to create a single national monetary system. Money and banking were left to the states, with the proviso that the states themselves could only make gold and silver legal tender. At the same time, there were no restrictions on private minters and private (free) banking. We should embrace this system again, repealing legal tender laws and letting everyone get into the business of the production of money. This would create a competitive market in which the best monies would emerge over time to compete directly with the federal government's dollar.

This system is ever more viable in an age of digital trading and communication. Everyone with an Internet connection now has the world financial system available at their fingertips. No longer should people be forced to use one money over another. Any and every monetary instrument should be made available to all. Let's put the power of free enterprise to work in the area of choosing which money is best.

It surprises me that even with all the legal restrictions on alternative money and payment systems many gold currencies are today thriving on the Internet, as well as complex private payment systems such as Paypal. The market will bring forth as many blessings in the area of monetary entrepreneurship as it does in all other goods and services. And it would be the same in banking. Banks would no longer be rewarded for leveraging deposits as high and long as possible. Soundness and safety would be the marks of successful banks, and their basis of profitability.

Ending the Fed need not be in one bold stroke. We could transition toward the goal. There are many small steps we can take toward sound money. The power of the Fed to increase the money supply could be curtailed. The Fed could be restricted in its open-market operations. We could, by legislation, deny authority to the Fed to monetize any debt. We could prohibit the Fed from participating in central economic planning.

We could stop the Fed bailout of its friends on Wall Street. We could have a true audit of the Federal Reserve and demand transparency for all its actions and collaborative plans with other central banks. Congressional authority to regulate the Fed should replace regulation of the financial markets. We would eliminate restrictions on starting new banks. We could permit alternative currencies. Those who want out of the monetary system should be protected by law. All taxes, sales, and capital gains must be removed from gold and silver when used as money.

The only way to bring about any of these changes is for the people to speak, and to speak clearly. Protests do a world of good. So does running for office. So does teaching the truth in high schools, home schools, colleges, and universities. Letters, seminars, articles, talk shows, all of these work to bring about political change. Educating yourself is the first step. (See my suggested reading list at the end of this book.)

Will we soon see the Congress, the courts, and the executive branch acting responsibly and working for a graceful transition to sound money? That is not likely. It did happen, under somewhat similar circumstances, with the Resumption Act of 1875, when we went back on the gold standard after it was suspended during the Civil War, and the return to gold was essentially a nonevent.

It's a different story today. We have a corporate welfare-warfare constituency demanding financing well beyond what could be paid for through taxes or even borrowing. The mentality is that there's no way we will give up our grandiose ideas of the role of government. The bailout psychosis that prevails prevents a sensible approach to transitioning away from the current deeply flawed system. Most people, especially those in Washington, still believe this system can be salvaged. They are wrong, and dangerously wrong.

We should work for reform and sound economics with a strict adherence to the Constitution, but, absent such change, we should be prepared for hyperinflation and a great deal of poverty with a depression and possibly street violence as well. The worse the problem, the greater the chance a war will erupt, especially as protectionist sentiments around the world grow. These are the wages of central banking.

Personal safety and economic security are our own personal responsibility. We can only hope that the government will not interfere in any effort of citizens to protect their families and their personal property.

I founded an organization called the Campaign for Liberty to bring like-minded people together. Efforts to pressure the government and politicians for positive change must continue, despite the pessimism that's sure to grow. I started the Foundation for Rational Economics and Education, which teaches economic liberty. I'm also a dedicated reader every morning of LewRockwell.com and Mises.org, the Web site of the Ludwig von Mises Institute, for which I serve as Distinguished Counselor.

Understanding the issues and how the free market offers the only answer to concerns about the well-being of our fellow man is crucial. Most supporters of big government are not malicious but are misled. Intellectually and compassionately explaining the reason freedom works is required for credibility. But first we must learn those reasons well ourselves. And that is entirely in our own hands.

The most encouraging part is that truth is on the side of liberty. Prosperity and social well-being are never a consequence of government's running the economy or regulating personal behavior. Our goals can only be achieved with a society that respects and equally protects the rights of every human being, old and young, rich and poor, regardless of gender, color, race, or creed. We must reject the initiation of violence by individuals or governments as morally repugnant.

A coalition of various political and educational groups to end the Fed is achievable and practical. During the 2008 presidential campaign, I organized a press conference in Washington, D.C. Four candidates agreed on a statement:

> We insist that there be a thorough investigation, evaluation and audit of the Federal Reserve System and its cozy relationships with the banking, corporate, financial institutions. The arbitrary power to create money and credit out of thin air behind closed doors for the benefit of special interest must be brought to an end. There should be no bailouts of corporations and no corporate subsidies. Corporations should be aggressively prosecuted for fraud.

The fact that this diverse group agreed to these four points, as well as a strong statement against the Federal Reserve, is quite significant. Principled people, no matter what group they identify with, are strongly inclined to challenge the power of the Fed. This includes liberals, conservatives, libertarians, progressives, and populists. Such a broad-based group can have an impact on bringing about change. With the financial system in shambles, people are open to reform. We have the opportunity for a strong intellectual and political campaign challenging the Federal Reserve to be heard.

Among all the arguments that can be used to reject the Federal Reserve, the moral argument alone should suffice. It's cheating. It's a tax. It's counterfeiting. It benefits the few at the expense of the many. It breaks the rule of contracts. It causes suffering and punishes the innocent. It enables world wars and vast payoffs to the powerful. That should be enough for all Americans to call for an end to this ninety-five-year-old failed scheme.

What is left for us to do? The future looks bleak. The power elites are hunkering down, and there's no sign that anyone in Washington cares, listens, or understands the issue of money and the power of the Fed. Does that mean our only option is to go into survival mode? I don't think so. There's a rumbling in the heartland, and anger is building. Harnessing that anger and converting it into positive and constructive energy could have favorable consequences beyond our imagination. It's time to become energized, not despondent, over the tragic mess that has been imposed on us.

We have a natural, God-given right to our lives, our liberties, and the fruits of our labor.

Protecting those rights is the only role that government ought to have in a free society. To restrain the government from doing more requires a morally determined people willing to assume self-responsibility, rejecting dependence on government force to mold the economy, society, or individual behavior.

If the freedom movement continues to grow as it has these past two years, I would say there's plenty of room for optimism. Freedom and central banking are incompatible. It is freedom we seek, and when that precious goal is achieved, the chant "End the Fed!" will become a reality.

SUGGESTED READING

Beginning

Greaves, Percy. *Understanding the Dollar Crisis* (Auburn, AL: Mises Institute, 2008, 1973).

Paul, Ron, and Lewis Lehrman. *The Case for Gold* (Auburn, AL: Mises Institute, 2007, 1983).

Rothbard, Murray N. *The Case Against the Fed* (Auburn, AL: Mises Institute, 1994).

Rothbard, Murray N. *What Has Government Done to Our Money?* (Auburn, AL: Mises Institute, 2005, 1963).

White, Andrew Dickson. *Fiat Money Inflation in France* (Auburn, AL: Mises Institute, 2008, 1896).

Intermediate

Mises, Ludwig von. *Causes of the Economic Crisis* (Auburn, AL: Mises Institute, 2006).

Rothbard, Murray N. *America's Great Depression* (Auburn, AL: Mises Institute, 2009, 1963).

Rothbard, Murray N. *The Mystery of Banking* (Auburn, AL: Mises Institute, 2008, 1983).

Sennholz, Hans F. *The Age of Inflation* (Belmont, MA: Western Islands, 1979).

Sumner, William Graham. *A History of American Currency* (Auburn, AL: Mises Institute, 2008, 1874).

Advanced

Hayek, Friedrich A. *Choice in Currency* (Auburn, AL: Mises Institute, and London: Institute of Economic Affairs: 2009, 1976).

Hülsmann, Jörg Guido. *The Ethics of Money Production* (Auburn, AL: Mises Institute, 2008).

Mises, Ludwig von. *The Theory of Money and Credit* (New Haven, CT: Yale University Press, 1953).

Rockwell, Jr., Llewellyn H. (ed.). *The Gold Standard: An Austrian Perspective* (Auburn, AL: Mises Institute, 1992).

Soto, Jesús Huerta de. *Money, Bank Credit, and Economic Cycles* (Auburn, AL: Mises Institute, 2008, 2006).

Bonus Reading

Murphy, Robert. *The Politically Incorrect Guide to the Great Depression* (Washington, D.C.: Regnery, 2009).

Woods, Thomas E. Jr. *Meltdown: A Free-Market Look at Why the Stock Market Collapsed, the Economy Tanked, and Government Bailouts Will Make Things Worse* (Washington, D.C.: Regnery, 2009).

For these and other books on the Fed and money, write for a free book catalog to the Ludwig von Mises Institute, 518 West Magnolia Avenue, Auburn, AL 36832 (334-321-2100; info@mises.org, www.Mises.org).